MY NEXT STEPS: CREATE A COUNSELING CAREER YOU'LL LOVE

Kate Walker, PhD, LPC, LMFT

My Next Steps: Create a Counseling Career You'll Love
By Kate Walker, PhD, LPC, LMFT
© 2017 Kate Walker
ISBN: 978-1-937514-72-3

Editorial Director: Dr. Larry Keefauver
Text Design: Lisa Simpson
Printed in the USA

Printed by:
Camden House Books, LLC
Post Office Box 727
Broken Arrow, OK 74013
GetMyNewBook.com
CHB-4538

All rights reserved solely by the author. The author guarantees all contents are original and do not infringe upon the legal rights of any other person or work. No part of this book may be reproduced, stored in a retrieval system, or transmitted in any form or by any means without expressed written permission of the author.

As a professor, I teach my students information from textbooks and research journals. This book gives them a real world understanding of what life is like as a professional counselor. Kate Walker's experience as a counselor, supervisor, and business owner is a valuable resource for those entering the profession or looking for a way to rejuvenate their career. The variety of experts she has chosen to include in the book is an excellent demonstration of the diversity in the field. The book is filled with practical information presented in way that allows the reader to see Kate's fun personality and passion for the field.

Le'Ann Solmonson, PhD, LPC, CSC
Professor, Director of Counselor Education, Student Affairs, and Higher Education, and Rehabilitation Services Programs,
Stephen F. Austin State University
Past President, Texas Counseling Association

Much like our clients do, Kate lets us into her world to find our own motivation for helping others. Walker and her group of experts present the honest dialogue of personal struggles one can face while noting how barriers to success can be overcome with continued work and effort. The words of encouragement, growth activities, tips, and suggestions provided will prove to be helpful for those who are considering a career in counseling and professional counselors who want to revitalize themselves and their careers. There is a great meaning and purpose in counseling- this book can help our future and current counselors get there and find it again!

Teri Ann Sartor, PhD, LPC-S, NCC, CHST
Assistant Professor of Counseling,
Lamar University

This book is a wonderful addition to counseling literature. The title does well in setting the tone to describe the book's contents. It incorporates rich and varied current trends, knowledge, skills and practices. Nicely done!

Brenda Jones, PhD, LPC, NCC, CSC
Clinical Assistant Professor,
The University of Texas at San Antonio
President, Texas Association for Counselor Education and Supervision

Kate has been dedicated to the counseling profession on multiple levels and has served as a trusted source for both practitioners and supervisors for many years. I highly recommend her book for novice or aspiring counselors and also for experienced professionals looking to re-invigorate their career

Paul Carrola, PhD, LPC-S, NCC
Assistant Professor, Mental Health Counseling Clinical Coordinator,
The University of Texas at El Paso
Senator, Texas Association for Counselor
Education and Supervision

If you are interested in becoming a counselor or creating a private practice, this is the guide for you. In her book, My Next Steps, Kate shares her expertise on how to create a balanced practice while avoiding career ending pitfalls. My counseling students and supervisees often ask about the business side of the profession and up until now there was no guide for them. Kate's book helps those thinking of becoming counselors, counselors in training, supervisees, and seasoned counselors who may need to re-evaluate some of their professional practices. Pick this book up today!

Angie D. Wilson, PhD, LPC-S, LSOTP, NCC
Assistant Professor,
University of North Texas
Past President, Texas Association for
Counselor Education and Supervision

Everything written in this book came from professionals with touching life experiences and clinical expertise. It is inspiring, hopeful, practical and doable. Also, it is designed for anyone who needs some wisdom and tools to proceed with the journey to their career.

Yu-Fen Lin, PhD, LPC-S
Assistant Professor, Internship Coordinator,
Counseling Program Coordinator,
University of North Texas Dallas

This book is a must have for both the novice starting their counseling career and the seasoned clinician who wants to take their practice to the next level. Dr. Walker does the same thing in writing this book that we are expected to do as counselors. She equips us with the necessary tools and motivates us to use them to be successful in our counseling careers. Thank you, Dr. Kate Walker!

B. J. Barksdale, MA, LPC-S, NCC
BJ & Associates, PLLC
Past President, Texas Counseling Association

"My Next Steps: Create a Counseling Career You'll Love," is a powerful guide for counselors, but equally powerful for those in the coaching industry. Kate's practical wisdom gently lights the path for professionals to gain clarity, remove fear, and take immediate action.

Dawn D. Mitchell
Author of *Light After a Layoff*

I needed this practical guide for myself and for giving career guidance to potential counselors over my forty years of counseling and guidance. This hands-on book is priceless wisdom and practical guidance for those just starting to actualize their dream, or needing to reboot an important area of their counseling practice. A must read!

Dr. Larry Keefauver, DMin
Founder of Your Ministry Counseling Services (YMCS)

Dedication

For David, Kyle, Ridgley, and Sarah

Acknowledgements

I am filled with humility and gratitude. When I think of all the people to thank for helping me make this book, it is hard to know where to start. To my husband David, thank you for loving me and walking with me on this adventure, even though you are on the other side of the world right now. I am grateful to Dawn Mitchell for holding my hand and getting this book out of my head; to my kids who are the reason I strive to achieve balance and make a living; and to Amber Haygood for holding down the fort and keeping the practice going while my I was trying to meet deadlines and birth this book. I am indebted to Sheila Gerth and Tammy Gross; two women who never met, yet over the decades and countless cups of coffee helped me make sense of my turmoil and turn it into stories.

I am grateful to friends who loved and nurtured me, and pushed me to stop working and get a workout, a pedicure, or a margarita. You know who you are. Thank you to the experts whose stories inspired me to write this book and to my mentors whose inspiration lit the fire under me and drove me to accomplish all that I have. A special thank you goes to my mentor Dr. Judy DeTrude. With a simple invitation to join you in private practice you changed my life. I will never be able to repay you for all you taught me about counseling, about being a professional, a supervisor, and a person of excellence. I still tell every class I teach, that if I don't know the answer I will call you. I'm still thinking about making those "What would Judy do?" bracelets. If I can be half the educator you are, I will consider my life well lived.

Table of Contents

Preface 13

Introduction 15

Chapter 1: Do It Right the First Time................................ 21

Chapter 2: Meet the Experts 29

Chapter 3: Your Story Is Your Strength 37

Chapter 4: Mitigating Mistakes.. 63

Chapter 5: The Therapeutic Use of Money........................ 81

Chapter 6: Make Time.. 95

Chapter 7: Achieve Balance 107

Chapter 8: Private Practice Primer 121

Final Word: The Lasting Benefits of Being a Counselor........... 153

About the Author 157

Preface

SAVE THE WORLD WITH BETTER THERAPY
(AND SAVE YOURSELF WHILE YOU'RE AT IT)

My story narrates how one therapist set out to save her son, and ended up becoming an asset to her community, her clients, her family, herself, and if we believe the butterfly effect, the world. She did it by choosing to become a professional counselor and help hurting individuals and families, teach others, and give away her time.

If you are reading this book you probably have a story too. If you are a fully licensed counselor…*congratulations!* If not, that's okay; this book is for you too. You probably have a passion to counsel others, and the principles in this book can help you turn that passion into a career. If I do my job in equipping and motivating my readers, you will finish this book and possess concrete tools to create a career that will look eerily like the one you fell in love with.

What is my ulterior motive?

*The world needs more therapists:
those passionate people willing
to sit with hurting people
and create healing.*

Introduction

MY STORY

*He said thank you mom for fixing my clouded broken mind
but excuse me if I seem a little rude.
While I was missing my childhood,
my brother and my prime,
you enjoyed the convenience of my solitude.*
– Edwin McCain

My son and I had a long discussion about this book. The song lyrics at the top of this page describe my pain and guilt as I dove into beginning my doctoral program and starting a business while my son was in jail or rehab. I saw my son's teenage years as key to my back-story. Diagnosed with various 'disorders,' arrested for impulse control issues, and eventually sent to rehab, my son didn't really have what you'd call an idyllic adolescence. In the first edition of this book I told that story.

What I forgot, and this wise young man remembered, is my story is really our story. While I was confused and sad about his choices and diagnoses, he was struggling with medications that left him confused about his body and distrustful of his mind. I struggled with the death of my mother but at the same time he was struggling with the fact his biological father wouldn't have contact with him. We both reeled emotionally from the deployment of my husband, his stepfather, to Iraq.

The long and short of it is none of us, not he, not I, not his sisters, not my husband, got out of the last twenty-six years without a story.

So I'm going to tell you my story and how it affected my journey to becoming a counselor. Maybe someday he'll tell you his.

Entering Counseling

In 1998, I started my master's degree in counseling. We had just received the first (of many) alarming notes home from my son's Kindergarten teacher; I was flustered, defeated, and taking it all *very* personally. I had been thinking about counseling as a career change and my son's issues gave me an added push to give it a try. In my first marriage, his biological dad had abused me. I had long thought that entering the counseling field would allow me to help other women trapped in violent relationships.

Since my son was having issues, I thought I could add to my skill set the ability to "teach parents how to control their out-of-control kiddos." Yes, 1998 was an idealistic year for me.

By 2000, I had my master's degree in counseling, but I wasn't quite ready to quit my day job. That was probably a good thing. Soon after 9-11, my husband mobilized with his Army reserve unit for almost twelve months, I had our third child, and I was working full time as an orchestra teacher. As a joke, I called myself the "counseling orchestra teacher" although I hadn't practiced a minute since finishing my degree.

By 2004, my husband was back home, and I was ready to start accruing licensing hours. However, I put off my decision to start practicing by doing what so many of us do—stay with what's safe and secure. I kept my teaching job and went back to school. As I think back, we were probably in between escapades with my son. Sam Houston State University was offering a fabulous deal so they could get their new PhD program off the ground (I really wanted that trip to Mexico they were offering) and it was only a couple of nights a week. To top it off, my husband was home from his mobilization so he could help with the kids and I could keep teaching. In other words, it seemed like a good idea at the time.

As life would have it, two months into my program my husband was mobilized to Iraq. Six months in, I was diagnosed with breast cancer. My son, well, you know what was happening with my son. So, I did what any logical person would do: I quit my teaching job and went to school full-time (you're welcome Sallie Mae). Six reconstruction surgeries, three years, and one dissertation later, I was ready to call myself "doctor" and open www.achievebalance.org, my cash-only counseling practice in The Woodlands, Texas.

Has it been smooth sailing since then? Heck no. But today my husband is mobilized with the Army in Poland. My beautiful son is free, supporting himself, and working. My middle daughter is at the University of North Texas and is a vocal advocate for the LGBTQ community and women's rights. My third child is fifteen and playing lots and lots of volleyball. The point is, and this is the takeaway from this book by the way, I didn't quit. I may have slowed down and I might have been driven by ego rather than passion; but I didn't quit. I have discovered that when a life's purpose has been deposited in you, the only way you can fail is if you quit. Now, almost fifteen years later, I am so glad I didn't.

My desire is that this book will keep you from procrastinating, making excuses, being distracted or simply quitting.

If you have passion to help and counsel others, and you are looking for a way to direct it,

this book is for you.

If you have lost your passion to help others heal and are looking for tools to re-ignite it,

this book is for you.

If you have fallen in love with a career focused on helping and healing others,

this book is for you.

If you need to overcome lack of confidence and fear of failing to actualize and do what you love,

this book is for you!

In the following pages, I will…

- Highlight for you the practical, doable steps to become a counselor.

- Introduce you to experts and *explain exactly* how they succeeded so you don't have to recreate the wheel.

- Give you scripts, tools, and resources that will empower you to overcome fear, be able to make a sustainable income, and avoid burn-out.

- Equip you to "get the FUD" out (as one counselor I know calls it). Fear, Uncertainty, and Doubt is FUD. What you need is Confidence, Assurance, and Faith to implement your dream and actualize your passion.

- Provide you with self-talk and motivational truths that will birth hope and enthusiasm for your dream to counsel, help, and heal hurting people.

In a nutshell, I will help you create "the career you fell in love with." By the end of *"My Next Steps: Create a Counseling Career You'll Love,"* you will:

- Create new habits that will help you define and achieve your counseling career goals.

- Make good decisions (like picking the right grad school, interviewing the right supervisor, protecting yourself from litigation and complaints) before they become mistakes.

- Build a financial bridge that will take the fear out of following your counseling dreams.

- Erase bad habits that will steal your joy and hurt your clients (hello self-care).

By the end of *My Next Steps* you'll also understand why your gifts make you too important to lose to things like going broke, getting discouraged, burning out, or getting fired. Your story and your passion got you started; now learn the next steps to some good habits to help you create a counseling career you'll love.

Chapter 1

DO IT RIGHT THE FIRST TIME
Your Success is Important

It's common knowledge that deteriorating mental health confronts all of us as an increasing social problem. What you may not know is that the challenges surrounding how we effectively treat and help those with deteriorating mental health have been building for years. Let's explore some background history to better understand today's troublesome issues.

If you have seen the classic movie, *One Flew Over the Cuckoo's Nest*, you have become aware of the fabled "mental institution" or "insane asylum." This fictionalized portrayal is probably tame compared to what actually happened in those warehouses packed with individuals suffering from mental health disorders. Patients in institutions were abused, experimented on, raped, lobotomized, and robbed of their dignity. With advances in psychiatric medicine and evidence-based treatments, experts began to question the efficacy of mental institutions and posited that they might be, in fact, making the patients worse.

The Community Mental Health Act, signed into law by President John F. Kennedy October 31, 1963, shifted resources away from large institutions to smaller community-based treatment centers. Financial assistance in the form of grants were intended to help states construct Community Mental Health Centers (CMHC), designed to provide, at a minimum, five essential services:

- Consultation and education on mental health
- Inpatient services
- Outpatient services
- Emergency response
- Partial hospitalization

The grant attempted to fund 1,500 new community mental health centers nationwide. Additionally, in 1965, Congress passed the Medicaid Act. Not only did Medicaid offer higher reimbursement rates for community-based care, it excluded payments to mental health institutions. The Supplemental Security Income (SSI), passed a few years later, provided direct financial support for eligible individuals with mental illness living in the community.

Even though by 2009, the institutionalized population had declined by 98 percent and clients' civil liberties were protected better than ever before public mental health systems were, and remain, critically underfunded and understaffed. The results of shuttering institutions without expanding community-based funding have been staggering:

- The risk of homelessness, substance abuse disorders, suicide, and incarceration among mentally ill children, youth, and adults has increased.

- The nation's three largest public mental health providers are correction systems.

- As many as 70 percent of detained youth have a diagnosable mental disorder and 20 percent have a serious mental illness.

- Tens of thousands of families relinquish custody of their children to child welfare and juvenile justice systems each year in order to access mental health services that are otherwise unavailable in the community.[1]

In my home state of Texas, our problems mirror those at the national level. According to NAMI 2010 statistics, Texas spent just $35 per capita on mental health agency services in 2006. This was just 1.1 percent of total state spending that year. And true to the national statistics, in Texas the criminal justice system is our most reliable mental health provider. In 2008, approximately 37,700 adults with mental illnesses were incarcerated in prisons in Texas.

Overcoming Fear

In spite of the funding issues (and because of them), we desperately need counselors. Unfortunately, the task of becoming a counselor can be as daunting as the national mental health statistics. Potential counselors enter universities with dreams of helping, but the reality is, the job market doesn't offer much. In Texas, we see LPC Interns with a forty-eight or sixty-hour master's degree facing a job market in which they cannot bill insurance for their time. As a result, they either compete with bachelor's level Qualified Mental Health Providers for low paying positions, or volunteer. Fully licensed counselors are often overworked, underpaid, forced to do paperwork on their own unpaid time, placed in dangerous situations, and required by third-party payers to apply ineffective treatment modalities that are inconsistent with their training.

---

[1] https://www.ymadvocacy.org/the-community-mental-health-act-of-1963/

In private practice, the outlook is not much better. Once interns become fully licensed they face the daunting task of running a business, a skill that was missing from their counseling education. Opting to take third party payments from insurance means working with managed care and adapting to a medical model. Therapists' hands are tied as they are forced to only treat diagnoses insurance companies will pay or only implement interventions insurance companies approve. Because the cost per hour is usually lower, therapists must increase the volume of clients they see per week to meet the cost of overhead.

Yes, it is scary out there. Overcoming fear is important though, because fear is a constant. Fear tells you to wait, put your dream on hold, or make sure it's just the perfect choice before you do it. Fear whispers, "Don't do it at all; you might fail or you might get in trouble." The lies which fear or FUD conjure up in your mind may be something like this…

- *You don't have enough money.*
- *You don't have enough time.*
- *You aren't smart or talented enough to do it.*
- *You're all alone and nobody will help you.*
- *Even if you do get educated and licensed, nobody will hire you.*
- *Even if you get hired, you won't make a difference.*

Those voices will be your constant companions as you try to make a difference becoming a counselor. You just can't let fear drive. Remember, we need you…hurting people need you. Robert Schuller often quipped, *"Find a need and meet it; Find a hurt and heal it."* If that calling is on your life, don't run from it. Embrace it. Someone on the other side of your being equipped is waiting for you to answer the call!

Ask the right, best-informed/ experienced people for help. The best way to overcome fear is to ask for help. Who you ask is important because you will get different answers that may confuse you. For instance, if you ask your professor the best way to start a private practice, or how to find a good internship, or for information about the best way to become a counselor supervisor in Texas, you may be surprised. Many times, those of us in counselor education have never worked in an agency or have never operated a private practice. It is not uncommon for a university to hire a counselor educator from another state who may not know the Texas licensing rules.

> **Ask yourself...**
>
> - What irrational voices of fear am I listening to and why am I choosing to let them distract me?
> - Who are the best-informed people I need to ask to help me?
> - Am I ready to move forward and stop procrastinating and making excuses?
> - How will it feel when I finally accomplish my dream and honor my calling to help others?
> - What is my next action step and when do I need to take it?

Take a moment and validate your feelings (that becoming a counselor seems scary, overwhelming, and expensive). Validation is important because if you don't validate your fear or plan for expenses, then you are setting yourself up to fail. The next few chapters will spell out exactly how to make this work. No guessing, no wondering where the missing pieces are, just tools that you can use to get from where you are, to where you are needed.

There is hope.

Our state has over fifteen universities with CACREP accredited counseling programs, over twenty-two thousand licensed professional counselors at this writing, and almost four thousand counselor interns and counselor supervisors. We have active state organizations, a legislature that is open to hearing us if we choose to speak, and one of the hottest business demographics in the United States.

There is opportunity.

Every day new sites appear on the internet offering endless opportunities for counselors to become excellent clinicians, healthier individuals, and successful business owners. And yet we are scared. Counselor supervisors are scared to train new counselors because they don't want the liability. Counselors are scared to move into private practice because they are scared to fail at business. School counselors are afraid to get licensed because they are scared of additional liability. We are scared, and we are just plain tired.

In this book I will inform you how practical, realistic principles will help make your mental health career more meaningful.

All of us need…

- **Passion…**passionate people who refuse to quit just because the going gets tough.

- **Excellence…**excellent people who won't do more harm than good because they make mistakes that can be avoided.

- **Generosity…**generous people who will give back, not just sell back, time because not every client has the means to get the help they need.

- **Balance…**balanced people who practice self-care because when you do become wildly successful we don't want to lose you because you worked yourself to death.

Right now, I am asking you to focus on this:

Believe that you have what it takes,
deep within yourself,
to make your counseling career dreams
a reality.

If you finish this book and decide it wasn't for you, all you've lost is some time doing your proper due diligence. But maybe if you can put your disbelief aside, you just might save (heal and deliver from hurt) the world around you.

Every dream begins with a dreamer.
Always remember:
You have within you
The strength,
The patience,
And the passion
To reach for the stars
To change the world.
—**Harriet Tubman**

 **Next Steps…**

At the end of each chapter, I will challenge you to think, feel, and do things that will move you forward in actualizing your dream to have the counseling career of your dreams.

1. Self-talk and ingrain in your brain these irrefutable truths...

   "I have the courage and strength to overcome my fears."

   Now write this on a post-it note on your bathroom mirror and say it out loud every morning and evening.

2. List the negative, distracting, and obstructive feelings you have now about actualizing your dream and then strike through them and overwrite them with the positive, empowering feelings you need to embrace to move forward. For example:

   ~~Fear~~ courage

3. Make a list of informed, experienced people you will reach out to for help, counsel, and guidance. Remember that when your pain of inaction becomes greater than your fear of failure you **will reach out for help!** Procrastination isn't an option.

   _____

   _____

   _____

   _____

4. Write it in your calendar. This might be the acceptance deadline for the counseling program you want to enter, the date of your licensing exam or, if you are already licensed, the date you will "make the leap" to pursue your supervisor designation, your private practice dream, or hire your first intern.

Chapter 2

MEET THE EXPERTS

Everyone wants to know how to do it "right." Whether right means avoiding mistakes, providing for a family, taking a day off, or just being happy in one's chosen career, doing it "right" can mean the difference between success and failure. I have talked with groups about everything: ethics, new laws, and best practices in counseling as well as answered a plethora of questions about doing it right. What I noticed is that some common themes emerged among the inquiries. Like the researcher I am, I decided to analyze them and discover, if I could, common denominators. Here's what I came up with in order of least important (number 5) to most important (number 1).

I've done it right if (drumroll please):

5. I have made enough money to provide for myself/my family.

4. I have the ability to take vacations and time off for family or sick days if I need to.

3. I am delivering excellent service to my clients and continually growing and learning.

2. I am not burned out.

1. I don't get a complaint filed against me.

While these themes were great, and they certainly represented the thoughts of hundreds of my fellow counselors, I wanted to dive deeper. My plan was to interview a small set of counselors currently working in agencies, non-profits, or private practice and find out how they were navigating the "doing it right" labyrinth. I chose one counselor to represent a large counseling practice/agency that takes third party payments; one counselor who runs an agency/non-profit; one counselor who operates a small cash-based solo practice; one counselor with small children who is utilizing interns to grow her practice; and finally, a counselor who owns a non-traditional multi-revenue stream counseling practice.

The interview consisted of fourteen questions:

1. What is your favorite quote?

2. What is something you love to do/hobby that has nothing (or very little) to do with your counseling job?

3. What is one thing you wish you could change about your:

   — daily schedule

   — weekly schedule

   — yearly schedule

4. Do you have a retirement plan?

5. What is your super power?

6. What is your favorite book to read?

7. What is something about you that not many people know and might even be surprised to know?

8. Are you a morning person or night owl?

9. What are three pieces of advice you would give someone starting in private practice?

10. What book most influenced you that you would recommend to others?

11. What is your "secret sauce"? Is it your morning routine? Your brand of coffee?

12. Do you meditate? How often and for how long?

13. Do you have another stream of income? If so, are you able to incorporate it into your practice?

14. What are the top two mistakes you made in your practice and how did you fix them?

These questions were fun and designed so my subjects would talk. I wanted to know about their fears, what they were proud of, and what they were reluctant to talk about. The results were amazing and the basis for much of this book. And talk? I was amazed at how they talked!

Their answers reminded me about why I got into this business in the first place. I learned so much. After each interview, I personally changed one thing about my practice in a positive way. This book is written so that you too can take their words and not just become a better counselor *someday*. It is written so that you can take your next right step and create a counseling career you'll love TODAY.

Our Experts:

Christopher S. Taylor, PhD, LPC-S is an adjunct professor of counseling ethics at Dallas Theological Seminary and Amberton University and the owner of Taylor Counseling Group (www.taylorcounselinggroup.com). As a graduate of Dallas Theological Seminary with a Masters in Counseling, Dr. Taylor utilizes existential psychotherapy to provide treatment for individuals struggling with loss of identity, depression, anxiety, and divorce recovery. As a Board-Approved Supervisor with a PhD in Counseling Education and Supervision, Dr. Taylor also provides supervision for licensed interns. In 2015, Dr. Taylor was appointed by Governor Greg Abbott to serve on the Texas State Board of Examiners of Professional Counselors as a professional member.

I included Dr. Taylor on our panel of experts because he owns and operates a large practice that accepts third party payments and employs several licensed professional counselors and LPC interns. Also, as a LPC Board member, he gives us an excellent perspective on counseling "the right way."

Following the murder of her son, Parris, **Dr. Katherine Bacon** founded the Parris Foundation in Houston, Texas (www.parrisfoundation.org). She currently serves as Executive Director. Katherine has served victims and the community for more than 16 years and is an active foster care alumna. Dr. Bacon is a Licensed Professional Counselor board approved supervisor (LPC-S) in

Texas and Nationally Certified Counselor (NCC). Currently she also serves as Region D Coordinator for the Texas Victim Services Association (TVSA).

Dr. Bacon is important to our expert panel because she is the owner of a nonprofit counseling agency in a large urban area, and like Dr. Taylor, she is an instructor and counselor advocate. Currently, she is an assistant professor of counselor education at a CACREP-accredited university, Texas Counseling Association's legislative liaison, and an avid researcher and grant writer.

Janet Nicholas MA, LPC, LCDC has been working with individuals and families for over twenty years. She completed her undergraduate studies in substance abuse services at St. Edward's University and her graduate degree in clinical psychology at Sam Houston State University. Janet is on our panel because she incorporates lots of different things into her counseling practice Trails Less Traveled (www.trails-less-traveled.com) and Janet Nicholas Counseling (www.janetnicholas.com). She is a licensed professional counselor, licensed chemical dependency counselor, a Christian counselor, and equine-assisted psychotherapist. In addition to counseling and conducting career assessments, she is a therapeutic placement consultant and author. Her first book, "Stepping Stones to A Healthy Stepfamily" was recently published and is available for purchase at Amazon.com.

Cheryl Butler, MA, LPC owns a small-and-growing practice, True North, that incorporates interns (www.truenorthtw.com). Cheryl is on our expert panel not only because of her rapid growth (she is adding two more interns in January 2018), but also because her dream is to provide a space that attracts skilled and passionate professionals who desire a balanced life where they can be home with their families.

She is the mom of twin seven-year olds and a three-year old. When she's not in the office, you will find Cheryl with her main loves: her three young boys and her husband (who is also a twin!). She embraces all aspects of being a "boy mom" (minus the mess) and believes that the home is the best classroom.

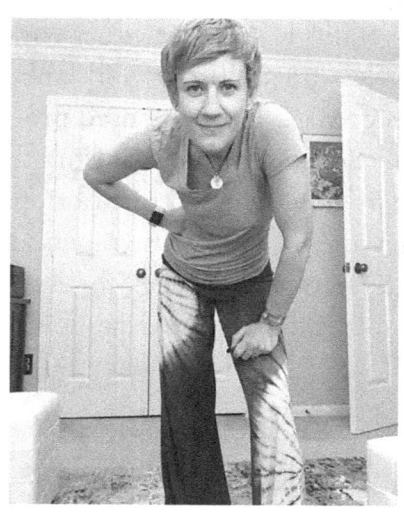

Jean Dixon, MA, LPC-S, CGP is a counselor, connector, encourager, and friend. A self-described "recovered woman," Jean is on our panel because she is the owner of a solo counseling practice (www.jeandixoncounseling.com), a master networker, inspiring blog author, and natural leader. She has created a very successful networking group for counselors, served as the president of the Houston Group Psychotherapy Association, and is a lifelong student of the spiritual and artistic. In her blog "The Golden Sparrow Flies" (www.jeandixoncounseling.com/golden-sparrow-flies/), Jean touches thousands of lives by chronicling her own recovery through eating disorders, food issues, and body acceptance.

Kate Walker, PhD, LPC/LMFT Supervisor. I included myself because I represent the counseling practice owner striking a balance among multiple interests and streams of income. At the time of publishing this book, I have a medium-sized counseling practice achievebalance.org that includes four licensed professional counselors in three offices, a full time salaried operations manager, and a graduate student (non-counseling) intern. My continuing education company Kate Walker Training provides continuing education and counselor supervisor training and just completed its thirty-first cohort of the LPC/LMFT forty-hour supervisor training. My nonprofit, Ann's Place, currently utilizes five interns to deliver affordable counseling to the South Montgomery County Texas community. In exchange for their counseling services, I provide my interns with free supervision. Finally, since I enjoy teaching, I am currently an adjunct instructor of marriage and family theories at Sam Houston State University.

All of these experts have something to teach you. Throughout this book, you will be able to listen and practice what they preach; all of us will help guide you in creating a counseling career you'll love.

Chapter 3

YOUR STORY IS YOUR STRENGTH

"I'm telling you he's not in Austin anymore," I said to the anonymous voice of the Houston Red Cross representative, "he's at… the APO address…I…gave you… in Iraq …." I was drawing my words out; stalling while I desperately looked up my Family Readiness Group (FRG) leader's phone number in Virginia. This was my husband's second mobilization. I had breast cancer and I was trying make a conference call with my FRG leader and the Red Cross representative who was trying to get him home before my surgery. "Hang on," I pleaded, putting my cell phone to my other ear, "I'm getting my FRG leader on the phone and she can verify everything I'm saying." A few more seconds passed, then the sound of the FRG leader's voice, "Hello?" That's when the sobs came. Like a child, I found myself spilling my story to two strangers, one of whom I knew only through our online support group, and neither of whom I would probably ever meet face to face.

But let me go back to the beginning. Our odyssey with the U.S. Army Reserves began with a blue Chevy truck. It wasn't ours yet, but it would be if we could come up with the down payment. Enter the U.S. army.

"Kate, this is only going to take one weekend a month and two weeks a year, and no one's been deployed since Desert Storm."

That's my husband Dave talking me into agreeing for him to come out of Individual Ready Reserve (a sort of inactive reserve status) and back into regular Army reserves.

"The detachment is in Huntsville, so I'll be close to home, and it's extra money," he said.

So we came away with the pretty blue truck and a six-year commitment to the 366th, a brand new military police detachment located in Huntsville, Texas. All was well in the Walker house. And then came September 11, 2001.

Worried teachers passed each other in the hallways as we snuck to the television in the teacher's lounge to grab glimpses of the world crashing around us. We wondered if the America we were teaching about would still exist at the end of the day. Forced smiles gave way to tears as I made it home and secured my own children in my arms. Dave and I stayed up all night watching the television and discussing his deployment that we both knew was now inevitable. The official call didn't come until three months later. I can still see the faces of my students as I struggled to understand what David was telling me over the hard plastic of my classroom phone pressed to my ear. "You leave in three days? One year, maybe two?" And with that, I was given the number of days I had left with my husband, and the approximate date of his return, God willing. I felt my stomach and there wasn't even a bump yet where a tiny heart was now beating. I realized that Bump might never get to see her father and that I might become a widow with three children. I turned around and finished my school day.

That was the pattern over the next three years and two deployments. I learned to tame my emotions and plan my crises. I experienced breaking down in the car on the way home, and needing to smile and hug my kids when the bus pulled up. I remember a news team coming to our house to do a feature story because Dave was one of the first reservists to be deployed from the Houston area. I happened to order pizza that night, and it arrived about the same time as the camera men and the perfectly groomed reporter.

"Dinner out of a box," he boomed, "The Walker family will be eating more of their meals from a box, now that their husband, their father, has been deployed."

I had no idea what pizza had to do with the possibility of never seeing my husband again, but like I said before, I had learned to time my emotional rifts. I put aside my confusion and prepared for my close-up.

The roller coaster ride of the reservist family! I had never been military before, so a husbandless/fatherless life was new to me. During his first deployment, I cringed every time I received an army family resource in the mail. What did they know about me? I wasn't in the army! I didn't sign up for this! I just wanted my husband back and coming home in his blue truck! Notes from the FRG hundreds of miles away about so-and-so's birthday, Christmas parties, Easter egg hunts, and baby showers only added to my sense of loneliness. Bump was growing within me into a very active Sarah, and her due date would come long before my husband's tour was over. By the miracle of Pitocin and a very understanding commander, when our beautiful third child made her entrance into the world, her daddy was there to catch her.

Fast forward with me to two years later. Remember my FRG leader on the other end of my cell phone in the first paragraph? By the end of that phone conversation, she and her husband (my husband's commander) had worked another miracle. Dave made it home two days before my mastectomy surgery and he stayed until I recovered enough to care for our children. Two years after that I finished my PhD and rebranded my counseling practice achievebalance.org and moved it to a brand-new area in a great demographic twelve minutes from my house. I had so many things that got me through those difficult times. Sometimes it was a wonderful attitude and good daily habits; most often it was simply wake up, pray, keep the kids and myself alive, and repeat. The next section of this chapter will describe the good tools and habits used by myself and my experts including attitude, visualizing success, boundaries, super powers, favorite books, and more.

Sustained by Attitude

If you are reading this book because you are planning to be a counselor, then you may have a story filled with challenges like mine. If you are already a counselor and you are reading this book looking for your next right step, then I'd say you definitely have a story like mine.

As a counselor, your story…

- is your strength and your compass.
- will remind and assure you that you know how to persevere when things get difficult.
- increases your empathy as you listen to clients and helps you connect.

Still, our stories cannot sustain us long-term. What more is needed? Amazing stories start us, but good habits and a positive attitude are what sustain us.

Attitude

When I graduated with my master's degree in counseling in 2000, I went right back to my teaching job. I was scared to make the leap. I knew I wanted to start a private practice someday but I was basically an introvert who knew nothing about business. Somehow, I learned about a cheesy-sounding book called *How to Win Friends and Influence People,* by Dale Carnegie. I thought, "I'm terrible at networking and I have no business skills. Might as well give it a shot," and dove in. As a broke teacher/post grad, it didn't hurt that the book was in the public domain and I could download it for free. I set up an office in an upstairs bedroom of my house, got my book, and did what I do best, started studying.

Holy moley, Dale Carnegie was a counselor. During this time in my upstairs office he taught me about:

- Developing confidence.
- Defining success.
- The importance smiling and making eye contact when talking with people.
- Forming friendships and remembering names of those who can refer you to others in need of counseling.

How to Win Friends and Influence People is such a non-counselor-sounding book. What you must understand is, it was written around the time of the second World War and joined other self-help books like Napoleon Hill's *Think and Grow Rich*. Their very straightforward messages (shake hands firmly but not too tightly) and no-nonsense titles were designed with a purpose.

> **Ask yourself...**
>
> - What do I need to do to build my confidence in taking the next step?
> - Who are the best-informed people I need to ask to help me?
> - On what date and at what time will I stop procrastinating and making excuses and take action?
> - What is my plan to focus, fight, and finish what's needed to go to the next level?
> - What is my next action step and when do I need to take it?

American farms had been decimated by the dust bowl and men had to find jobs in the city. World War II was coming to an end and men were coming home to compete for jobs and start families in the suburbs. These men had to learn how to survive in the post-agrarian economy and prosper. The premise was simple: change your mind, change your attitude, create opportunities, and successfully make enough money to support your family. I liked that.

Having the right attitude or mindset is important because without it you will lack motivation. You have a lot to do and there is no syllabus to guide and push you along.

- If you are going into private practice, you must complete the paperwork for your LLC or risk having a practice that is poorly protected against client lawsuits.

- If you are about to graduate, you must interview supervisors or risk having a dissatisfying or even dangerous supervision experience.

- If you just finished your forty-hour supervisor training you must develop an interview process to find quality interns who won't expose your practice to liability.

- If you are thinking about a graduate school to start your counseling career or,

- If you are making the leap from school counselor to LPC you must take time to choose the right school to pick up your licensing hours or risk delaying getting your license (or not getting it at all).

Don't let fear, uncertainty, and doubt keep you from moving from studying about counseling to "doing it." Refuse the urge to procrastinate. Focus on your goal. Fight through your distractions. Finish what you started with your school. The essence of the right attitude is this:

Now is the time to focus, fight, and finish.

Ask yourself and answer the questions in the sidebar on the previous page.

What if I told you the task in front of you (looking for schools, interviewing interns, etc.) would only take about six hours? Without the right attitude, it will be difficult to motivate yourself to set aside two extra hours over the next three days in order to do the work you need to do to get the results you want. Remember, your story and your passion only get you so far. Setting an intentional finish line and learning new habits lead to adjustments in time and resources (otherwise known as prioritizing) that will push you through to your next breakthrough. That's when the magic happens.

Lots of people describe this next part in different ways, but since I am writing for counselors and counselors in-training, I broke this "attitude adjustment" into three areas:

- Visualize
- Set Boundaries
- Get Gritty

Visualize

"I wonder what I will be when I grow up...?" In my years working with adults, I've found that this is a very relevant question. As we age, move away from home, love, and experience loss, that question causes a lot of angst. Understanding that we are not the same person we were when we were six, or twenty-two, or forty, we need to know why and how we have changed. From my personal observations, I am grateful our ideas about our identity change from childhood; otherwise the world would be filled with way too many ballerinas, princesses, and firefighters. So maybe for grownups, the question is not "What will I be when I grow up?" but rather, "What will define success for me tomorrow?"

Let's look at our lifestyle for answers. We struggle with our many identities and define ourselves in many different terms: "I am a mother...I am a wife...I am an employee." Sometimes others try to define us with terms like *workaholic*, *health nut*, or *Type A personality*. The most unpleasant definitions are usually the ones that catch us by surprise, like: "You are a diabetic," or "You are a ticking time bomb with your high blood pressure." And then one day it hits you and you ask yourself, "Have I become the person I intended to be?"

Your story gave you a beautiful picture of your calling. Now it is time to get laser-focused and to visualize the steps that will take you where you want to be. Don't worry, I will take you step by step so by the end of this book you will have a plan. Visualizing is important because success is personal.

Take a moment and think about what success might look like for you.

In ten years, if I am successful I will be able to say:

- ✓ *I am taking a vacation this year.*

- ✓ *I'm going to retire when I am 65.*

- ✓ *I'm only going to work half days now so I can spend more time with my kids.*
- ✓ *I love my collection of old Bentleys.*
- ✓ *I'm going to travel the world and manage my continuing education business from my laptop.*

Now you try to write it yourself.

"In ten years if I am successful I will be able to say…"

"_____"

"_____"

"_____"

Visualizing success might lead you to imagine a Bentley in your garage or beachfront condo. Success might also look like the ability to only work two days a week so you can spend time with your kids, or save $5000 in cash reserves in case you need to take a month off due to an illness or the death of a loved one.

Now think about how your ideal counseling career looks. If you are a new counselor or recent graduate, you might want to talk with other counselors or pay attention to the expert section in each chapter of this book. You will hear some great stories about what real counselors love the most about their job and their life. If you have been a counselor for a long time and feel burned out take a moment and try to connect with that passion, that story that brought you into this field.

Finish this sentence using the words from the word bank on the next page:

"I am a _____ and I help _____ who _____ with _____."

(Word bank: Counselor, helper, therapist, people, couples, kiddos, teens, struggling, working through, surviving, recovering, coping, don't get along, addiction, infidelity, their peers, family, trauma, cutting.)

Finally, think about your perfect counseling setting:

- ☐ Private practice full-time
- ☐ Private practice part-time
- ☐ Community Counseling Agency
- ☐ Hospital/general care
- ☐ Group home/children
- ☐ Clergy care
- ☐ Substance abuse inpatient and outpatient
- ☐ Residential geriatric
- ☐ Hospital/acute care psychiatric
- ☐ School
- ☐ Other

Write down what success looks like, the type of counselor you want to be, and your ideal setting and call it your "Counseling Success Plan." Be sure to write it in the present tense so it sounds like it is happening NOW. You can get creative and make a vision board or do like I did and just tape your Counseling Success Plan to your bathroom mirror. Say it out loud at least five times every day.

Just before you go to sleep, write these things and put the list face down next to your bed:

- ✓ Five things you are grateful for.

- ✓ ALL of your "A-ha" moments. Take your time with this; these will be the seeds for tomorrow's to-do list.

- ✓ Your accomplishments.

Go to bed and rest.

Set Boundaries

Remember a few paragraphs ago when I suggested it might only take about six hours to do the thing that will start your counseling success snowball rolling? Let's revisit that. Imagine that it will take the average person six solid hours to…

- ✓ Research supervisors and create good interview questions.

- ✓ Find a good lawyer or legal zoom document to create an LLC for a counseling practice.

- ✓ Call three universities and connect with the director of internships and let him or her know you are ready to take on some interns.

- ✓ Make a list of five possible appropriate graduate schools to start your counseling journey or finish your academic hours for LPC licensure.

You can divide up these hours however you like. The story goes that Theodor Seuss Geisel (Dr. Seuss) had a regimen where he wrote two hours each day, no more, no less. Author Cheryl Strayed on the other hand, who at the time she was writing her memoir "Wild," had two young kids, preferred locking herself in a hotel room for a couple of weekends and writing non-stop (I can totally relate to that). What I want you to remember is 80 percent of your productivity is determined by 20 percent of your effort. If you have only one hour each day, then you must work that entire one hour. If you do the "lock me away" method, then you must guard every minute. Welcome to the world of setting good boundaries.

Good boundaries are a part of any good relationship. The problem? They can be hard to enforce. The boundary-setter finds it hard because he dreads retaliation from the boundary-receiver. The boundary-receiver finds it hard because, well, no one really LIKES to receive a boundary. If you are a mom or a dad with young kids, you may need to lock a door (with the kids and your spouse on the other side) or spend ten bucks for an hour of babysitting time. If you are still working on a degree or have huge responsibilities with your job, then you may have to miss some deadlines or talk to your professor/supervisor/boss about your counseling dreams. If you are a Facebook addict, then there are TONS of great apps that will block social media while you get your work done. Long and short of it: you're going to have to make some uncomfortable changes.

When I started my PhD program, I was already used to the "two hours a day" productivity schedule. As a double bass music major at the University of Texas at Austin, I was expected to practice four hours a day. This of course meant I practiced a solid two. In 1999, I decided to run a mini triathlon to get back into post-baby number two shape and the only time I could train was two hours before the bus came for child number one. Upon making the decision to pursue a PhD, I knew if two hours per day was enough to make it through a triathlon and my bachelor's degree, it was enough to finish a PhD I would set my alarm for four, study or write until the kids woke up, get them off to school, then go to work and teach orchestra.

If you are a morning person like me, great. If you aren't and you plan on locking doors or purchasing hotel rooms, here are three things you need to know about boundaries:

Boundaries are designed to protect the boundary-setter (YOU), not the boundary receiver (kids, your spouse, your

supervisor, Facebook). Let's say you love your neighbor, you love your neighbor's cows, and you love your yard. You do not, however, love your neighbor's cows IN your yard. In fact, you are starting to lose your serenity over it. Since you value your yard and your serenity, you decide to build a fence. The cows are a little miffed because they can't get to your grass and your neighbor is a little miffed because his view is now marred by your fence. You, on the other hand, feel pretty good because you have your serenity and your yard.

Lesson: You built a fence because you value your peace more than your neighbor's peace.

Boundaries are not the same as telling someone what to do. Let's say you have the same neighbor, the same cows, and the same yard. You realize that a fence might hurt your neighbor's feelings so you are going to try some things that are "less offending" than a fence. Here's what you try:

- ✓ You try to talk to your neighbor and tell him that if he *cared about you* he'd keep his cows on his own side.
- ✓ You tell your neighbor that *it's just common sense* to keep his cows under control and if he had any common sense, he would do that.

Lesson: Nagging, guilt trips, and melt-downs, are attempts to change or control another person. These efforts rarely protect your serenity, and they always damage relationships.

Boundaries will always require a change in *your* behavior, not your neighbor's. Did the neighbor have a right to graze his cows on your grass? *No.* Did you have a right to be angry? *Sure.* Is it fair that you had to spend money and time and energy to build the fence when *his* cows are the problem? *Yes.* After all, you care more about your serenity (and your yard) than your neighbor does.

Lesson: If you value it, then it's up to you to protect it.

Once you have set your boundary and time limit, make a to-do list of what you intend to accomplish. It's okay if this is a long list; you probably won't accomplish everything. Here are three simple steps to be super productive for two hours:

- Write down three things and three things ONLY from your to do list and place it where you can see it. Put your to-do list away.

- Finish the three things.

- Go back to your to-do list and grab three more things. Repeat.

Boundary setting is important not only for your future vision, but also for your well-being. Counseling requires 100 percent emotional engagement with our clients. Counselors divide this emotional engagement into one hour increments every day. If you have a family, you will emotionally engage them when you are home. Friends, clients, family, traffic, what you ate for lunch this afternoon, will all compete for your emotional attention. Without good boundaries, you and those relationships will suffer, and your job will get tougher.

Get Gritty

You know grit is quite a hot topic these days (check out Angela Duckworth's grittiness research at https://angeladuckworth.com/media/). Grit means you go through a hellacious experience and you do more than just survive, you thrive. Or perhaps you are the Energizer bunny and no matter what happens, you just keep going and going and going. My own gritty experiences (I think the actual word I used to describe them at the time only rhymed with gritty) involved getting a cancer diagnosis, having three little kids, knowing my husband was in a combat zone, and deciding to start a PhD program and a new counseling practice. What are the five traits of *getting gritty*? They are...

- Courage
- Achievement
- Follow-through
- Excellence (rather than perfection)
- Grittiness

Courage, or your ability to manage fear of failure, can only be cultivated through hardship. That's a tough sell. Most of us would rather learn courage from a textbook than a hardship.

Achievement might seem like an easier virtue to swallow. A note to all of you perfectionists out there: this is NOT meticulous, conscientious, completion. It is a "do-your-best/finish-it-up/get-on-to-the-next-task-whether-it-looks-pretty-or-not" virtue. Good-bye analysis paralysis.

Follow-through is akin to the 10,000 hours to mastery Malcolm Gladwell made famous in his book "Outliers." To follow through means you wake up and keep going. Whether you spend two hours or ten minutes, daily practice with purpose is the driver behind accomplishing long-term goals. Much like resilience, follow-through can be described as the belief that "everything will be alright in the end, and if it's not alright, it's not the end."

Excellence, is a gritty trait because it is not perfection; it is an attitude. In Seth Godin's book "Purple Cow," he reminds us that we are all artists with a gift that is a joy to produce and will make the world better. His message? Relish the joy of creating instead of focusing on how to perfect something for an audience.

Grittiness is important because you will need it when times are tough. If you fail your first try at your licensing exam, if your accountant tells you that you forgot to put aside enough money for taxes, if a disgruntled client files a complaint against you, you will need grittiness (the ability to know there is a light at the end of the tunnel even when you can't see your hand in front of your face) in order to persevere.

 **Next Steps…**

Read the following questions and answers in the next section: **The Experts Weigh In.**

After their comments, write your answer.

The Experts Weigh In

The first part of this chapter was about your story, your attitude, and how you visualize success. The second part detailed the tools like courage, achievement, resilience, follow through, excellence, and grittiness to help you get there. I'd like you to hear from our experts now. Their favorite quotes, super powers, and books will help you understand how they view life and success, accomplishment and motivation. It reminded me that having a sense of humor and the ability to laugh at yourself is also vital to success. Here are some of their answers to my questions.

What is your favorite quote?

Christopher Taylor: *I'm a huge Hemingway fan. My favorite quote as an aspiring writer, a very bad writer, I think, is, "There is nothing to write. You just sit down at your typewriter, and bleed." And that's been a big inspiration for me as I've tried to write things. What Hemingway was really talking about was that in his struggles to write anything meaningful, or what he felt was meaningful, he always felt that he got blocked by this drive to write something.*

And so he felt that if you were going to be a good writer, that you couldn't actually write. You just had to go experience the world, and then bleed that experience, and that emotion onto the page, which is really very powerful.

Cheryl Butler: *I have two and just couldn't decide. The first one is, "Comparison is the thief of joy," and it's probably my favorite. And then the other one is, "Wherever you are, be all there." Those are my two that I use all the time in my own personal life, and I share them with my clients.*

Katherine Bacon: *My favorite quote is, "If you are not a part of the solution, you are a part of the problem."*

Janet Nicholas: *That one was really hard because I am a quote freak. I love quotes, so I just picked one out of my book that I really love, because I love to use metaphors about road maps and about how life is so much about being on a journey. I really like this one by Elizabeth Elliot. It says, "Maps, road signs, and a few useful phrases are good things, but infinitely better is someone who has been there before and knows the way."*

Jean Dixon: *I have actually two favorite quotes. My overall favorite quote, because I'm a huge Tolkien, Lord of the Rings fan and Hobbit nerd, and we have it in our house is, "Not all those who wander are lost." I think of that in terms of myself, but also the clients that I work with. And the one that's been on my mind actually yesterday and today, but I really like it is, "In moments of doubt, trust your gut, hug your dog, and eat a donut." I just*

	really like that. I like donuts, I like dogs, I like trusting my gut. And I doubt a lot.
Kate Walker:	*My favorite quote? Like most of the others, I have two. One I just heard about a month ago and I put it into my weekly newsletter called "Friday Freebies." I think I was having a tough day just getting started so this quote by Chuck Close resonated with me: "Inspiration is for amateurs; the rest of us just show up and get to work." The other one was gifted by my dad. It was posted above our family weight room in our basement in the house where I grew up (yes my home was pretty boy-centric): "No pain, no gain."*

Your answer:

_____

_____

_____

What is your super power?

Janet:	*I'm a super-spiritual person, so my ultimate super power is God first, but I thought about that even more and I just saw "Wonder Woman." I was so blown away by her character. Of course, I liked it too, because it started out with horses, and I liked how they treated their horses in that movie, but I loved what a warrior she was and how naïve she was in so many ways, but she was a woman of truth and integrity and valor. So if it had to be somebody that was not God, it would be her.*

Cheryl: *You know, one really strange superpower is I remember peoples' names and faces forever and ever and ever. I will meet somebody again that I met maybe six years ago, and I will just know their name, and my superpower feels weird because then they look at me like, "I don't know you and you're kind of creepy." But I remember peoples' names forever and ever. So that's definitely one. I think discernment would be another one. I love being around people and I don't want to say reading people, but kind of just getting a feel for their heart; just a strong connection to people. I would like to think that another superpower I have is helping people not feel left out. I don't like when anyone feels left out or alone, so I love to be a connector. I think I'm good at connecting people together.*

Katherine: *Technology is my superpower. I cannot do everything I do without technology. It just would not be possible. So as much as I complained about the one thing I would change, about my schedule and how I would just love to unplug....technology does allow me to get things done.*

If I had to think about it in terms of me and my superpower, I would say I have a skill where I can see connections with things. So that is my own personal superpower... it's just a gift that I have. My brain just works that way. I can see connections between possible partnerships and resources, and networking opportunities, ways to collaborate and expand resources...In growing a business with small resources, being able to identify opportunities to stretch resources, that skill has been very, very helpful.

Jean: *My cool car and I actually wear superpower panties. You can buy them at Target. I won't tell you which ones I have on today.*

Somebody once told me in a group session I did, my superpower is me. I am superwoman. But I guess what I would say is that I'm really good at seeing and helping my clients see the signs in their life. If they could step back and really see that there is something larger leading them, they just need to see the signs to understand. So, synchronicities I think is my superpower. I'm really good at being able to connect...connect people, connect things, connect concepts, connect what things are there for us, and leading us. So, I think that's a superpower.

Christopher: *I can catch a flight…any flight. I would be on it.*

It was Fourth of July, but we still had Monday class because Fourth of July was on a Tuesday. The flights were different, and I didn't realize it, and I got into a routine of my flight being every Monday at 11:00. And so, I got into the routine of leaving the house at 10:15 to be at the airport to be on the flight. This particular day, I wake up, and I'm going through my normal routine, and I see that the flight is at 10:30. So I'm standing there and I'm like, oh man, do I call the class and just tell them, hey guys, I'm not coming, or do I try to make the flight?

I decided to go all in…and I make it from my house, leaving my house to boarding, walking on the plane as the last person, in 37 minutes. The drive itself is at least 30 minutes, but I made it in 20. And I mean not from my house to the airport, I mean from my house to walking on the plane. I was the last one on, when they closed doors right behind me. I was so pumped up, I actually wrote a short story about it on the plane

Kate: *My super power? I am an early to bed early to rise master. My coffee maker is set to 5:30 am and I love to open the* *curtains in my bedroom so I can see the sunrise and start writing. Before my hormones rebelled against me in my late forties, my additional super power was the ability to fall dead asleep at 9:30 pm the minute my head hit the pillow. It takes a little longer now, but I am still the daily dawn-greeter.*

Your answer:

_____

_____

_____

What is your favorite book to read?

Jean: *The book that I'll pick up a lot and is in my office is "The Book of Awakening" by Mark Nepo. He has several books, but this one is about when he developed cancer, and created his new concept of life. Each page is to be read for that day, if you want to do it that way, but you can just read the section. It's just how he thinks a lot differently. So, "The Book of Awakening" is how he awakens. I'll find myself picking that up quite often for either inspiration or connection…it's delightful.*

My most gifted or recommended book is "Eating in the Light of the Moon" by Anita Johnston. It's about letting go of the log that keeps you from swimming. It's told through metaphors. We use it a lot with eating disorders even though those words are never used in the book. So, the idea of letting go of the log, your security, and everybody's saying, "Hey swim," and you're like, "I got this log, and this log is keeping me up. So, I've got to keep this log." It's through metaphor…teaching women about recovery, but

> *I use it for a lot of different things. It's a pretty powerful little book.*

Christopher: *I don't really know that I have many books that I go back to and re-read regularly, but I'll tell you the most influential books of my life are definitely by Hemingway. I like "For Whom the Bell Tolls." That is an amazing book, and I think one of the best endings in American literature. "The Strange Case of Dr. Jekyll and Mr. Hyde" I really enjoy…I've read it a few times…It's so good, and the story behind it is really fun because Stevenson wrote it to pay off a gambling debt. He wrote it on a train ride. I use the themes in that book regularly in therapy. And then, the book that changed my life, Søren Kierkegaard's, "Fear and Trembling." So those would be some of my favorites.*

My most recommended book for fellow entrepreneurs, or individuals that want to build something, is Gino Wickman's book, "EOS: The Entrepreneurial Operating System," which is a really good book. I would suggest "Good Grief," for anybody's who's experienced loss.

Katherine: *I have several. It really depends on what's going on in my life at the time, but I'm a big Harry Potter fan… books that allow me to indulge in fantasy, but also have an element of moral lessons. I'm a very systemic person, so I like things that deal with different systems… fantasy with something tied to real-life metaphors.*

I will tell you the most recent book that I read for myself for fun was Trevor Noah's "Born a Crime." I read that over the holiday break. That was my gift to myself. I totally unplugged for a couple of days, and I just buried myself in a book, and that was what I read. It was great. It was heavy, a little hard to read at times. I over-identified with it in some places, but it was a really great book. So sometimes, I'll read books like that.

I don't have a specific book that I recommend, but what I would say has been the most helpful for me ... As I realized that I couldn't do it by myself, and I had to establish a team, I started reading books, mostly textbooks, or pseudo textbooks. I started reading books on human resource development. Human resource development is a profession that blends human resources, counseling, and career training within several different disciplines very nicely for what I needed to know.

I needed to know, how do I identify the right types of people to join the team? How do I help them become a small team, and how do I empower them to take ownership of the team, so I don't have to be the one that's doing all of that? I can't be that person for everyone, all the time, and so reading books on HRD helps me. I've read great stories from CEOs on how they established healthy teams. So, it wasn't teams of counselors, it was just establishing healthy teams, but I had to then take and apply those concepts to establish a team of counselors.

And also, I had to establish a team of counselors that had team members who are business people. How do I create a team of counselors that also has an accountant, and an executive, and IT person, and a web person? I need everybody to understand each other, so they can work well together.

And so, books on HRD have just been very, very helpful for me to develop those skills that I needed to do that, and strategies on how to create that type of culture and environment.

Cheryl: *The most recent favorite book I had was called "Nightingale" and I don't remember the author, but it was fantastic. It's historical fiction, and it's beautiful.*

I actually wrote down four books I recommend to others. Two of them are in the same category. One is "Parenting from the Inside Out." It is a fantastic read. I love it for parents, who can then kind of do some self-reflection about what's going on in their world and how it affects how they're parenting. Then the second category, I love "Stop Walking on Eggshells" and "I Hate You, Don't Leave Me." And the third is "Raising Grateful Kids in an Entitled World." That's one of my recent reads that I remember, and it's a great parenting book for families who are struggling with overindulgence and abundance, which we have a lot of in our area.

Janet: *I'm going to make a confession here, I am a book addict, and I don't want to be in recovery for that [laughing]. I love, love, love reading. I have my whole entire life. I love anything by C.S. Lewis, but this young woman is kind of like a modern-day female C.S. Lewis, and I've not read anything as profound. The way I describe it is, to me it was almost like eating decadent chocolate, and I would only read a few pages a night because I didn't want to rush through this book, it was so beautifully written, and it really changed my view about gratitude. Her name is Ann Voskamp, and the book is called "The Greatest Gift." It was a really profound book. The other book that I really love as a therapist is by Dr. Dan Siegel. That book is a powerhouse.*

My most recommended book? For years, I have loved "Boundaries" by Drs. Cloud and Townsend, so even people that are not coming from a spiritual side, that book has taught so many people, and it's the kind of book that you could re-read every year and get something new out of it. I've seen a lot of lives changed with that book. I also love anything by Brene Brown. Absolutely love Brene Brown.

My old, old staple is "Co-Dependent No More" by Melody Beatty, another book that has transformed lives, and it seems to be that no matter whether you're a young person or a more mature and older person, that book resonates with so many people.

Kate: *My favorite books right now? Everything my experts recommended of course! One of the wonderful outcomes of this project are all of the new books in my Kindle library. I will read anything science fiction and fantasy or suspense. I call it brain candy. I also enjoy memoirs like Cheryl Strayed's "Wild," and right now I am reading a book by noted physicist Richard Feynman "Surely you're joking Mr. Feynman! Adventures of a Curious Character." Regarding books I recommend, I make every intern who I agree to supervise read the following: "Hold me Tight," by Sue Johnson, "Surviving an Affair," by Willard F. Harley Jr., "How to Help Your Spouse Heal from Your Affair: A Compact Manual for the Unfaithful" by Linda MacDonald, "Addictive Thinking," by Abraham Twerski, "Dance of Anger," by Hariett Lerner, and "No More Mister Nice Guy," by Robert Glover. Many of those I recommend to clients as well.*

Your answers:

_____

_____

_____

My Next Steps: Create a Counseling Career You'll Love

Chapter 4

MITIGATING MISTAKES

You're my favorite mistake.
– Sheryl Crow

Talking about our personal mistakes can be difficult. I could do a presentation about five ways to make your counseling practice better or the top three things to help you succeed in your counseling career. However, I have learned that talking about mistakes will accomplish so much more toward improving your practice.

First, hearing me and the other experts describe common mistakes and how we fixed them will help you understand that mistakes are a part of the process, and there is almost always a way back from them. Second, it's always helpful to see the train coming. Knowing what to expect will help you prepare. Finally, mistakes are only harmful if you never learn from them. I won't present a mistake or scary situation in this chapter unless I can also give you a way to mitigate the damage.

Becoming a counselor and creating a career you'll love is not the same as developing muscle memory for a golf swing, increasing endurance for a triathlon, or any other sports-related skill for a sports-related activity. If it was, I'd be advising you to, "Get in the game before you're ready!" and, "Get injured!" *Why?* Because in counseling you must:

1. *Recognize mistakes are inevitable and stop being afraid of them.*

2. *Mitigate the fear of making a mistake by maintaining an emergency fund, a network of consultants you can call on, and a sound decision making model.*

3. *Persist. Never quit. Don't give up.*

Like most of you, I started my practice as a solo practitioner. Within five years I added a continuing education component, a non-profit, and several new therapists from whom I took a percentage of their profits (fee-splitting). Unfortunately, taking a percentage of another therapist's income, while one of the most profitable components of my practice, was also unethical.

When I recognized that fee-splitting was not the proper way to make money in private practice I dropped that component like D'Onta Foreman dropped the ball in the UT versus Texas Tech football game in 2016. It was a HUGE blow to my income and my ego. If I hadn't had an emergency fund I don't think I would have survived and thrived.

After ten years in practice, I am on the constant hunt for systems, software, gadgets, and hacks to ethically streamline my practice, save time and money, and increase profit and life balance. My father who passed away in 2014, was a super hero to me and he kept a sign above the family weight room that read, "No Pain - No Gain." In business, if you aren't willing to accept that there will be some pain (making mistakes, losing money, wasting time) you will never get to experience the gain.

My goal for this chapter is to describe common mistakes, explain why they are mistakes from an ethical, legal, or professional stance (or a combination of all three), and then give you practical tools to tackle these issues in your own counseling setting. I describe different situations for different levels of licensure. My hope is that you will take away concrete ideas you can implement today so you can avoid mistakes and if you can't avoid them, you can get them fixed quickly.

Choose Your Supervisor Carefully

I enjoyed meeting with Marvin. He liked to meet me at cool places where we could drink coffee and talk about counseling. I was newly graduated and he promised me he would help me get my private practice off the ground. He had big plans for a big practice, and he was willing to take me on as his intern. This sounded like it was right up my alley! I asked around about Marvin and my intern colleagues seemed to like him. That was the extent of my research, and I signed my name on the dotted line. In a few weeks I was officially his intern.

> **Ask yourself...**
> - What traits am I looking for in a supervisor?
> - Who can refer me to excellent supervisors?
> - What criteria do I need to establish for doing in-depth due diligence when choosing a supervisor?
> - Are there jobs that offer free supervision?

The first intern meeting was a blast. Several of my classmates from school were there and we all had our pens and paper ready to learn all we could from this smallish man with a beard in his mid-century modern (that's what he called it) office in the heart of our bustling community. He was smart too. He told us how he had read all of the books on his bookshelf and those of us considering a PhD were just wasting our time and money. We wrote our checks and scheduled the next supervision.

The weeks went by and finally one of us spoke up. Would we be seeing clients soon? Marvin was charging us for supervision and also for using his administrative assistant, his phone, and a portion of his office. There had to be about twelve of us; I could see that what we were paying wasn't what we were getting. We found out the majority of his clients were insurance pay and he didn't have enough cash-pay clients to keep us all busy. He had discouraged us from having other sites. His expectation was for us to pay our/his office bill and his supervision fee, even though we weren't seeing any clients for him to supervise. I think it took me about three months before I finally had the nerve to call him and terminate our supervisory relationship. I wrote a letter to the board to make it official.

As hard (and expensive) as it was for me to learn, I will never forget the feeling of being taken advantage of by someone who I thought that by virtue of his title and license, had my best interests at heart. Dr. Li, my amazing former professor at SHSU, agreed to be my new supervisor. He took me through my three thousand hours, and I emerged as a licensed professional counselor and licensed marriage and family therapist. My internship included a private practice and a chronic pain center. I had no trouble getting my client hours completed. Yes, I paid Dr. Li for his supervision time, but his fee was reasonable and the experience was invaluable.

Choosing your supervisor carefully is important because he/she will help you grow from being a knowledgeable master's degree holder to a talented license holder. Although I had to start over with Dr. Li, staying with Marvin would have made the mistake much worse (and much more expensive). I might have even quit the profession. If you are a new therapist, take your time and find a good supervisor. If you are already licensed, then BE a good supervisor. Some good interview questions for a potential supervisor are:

1. *How many years have you been supervising?*
2. *How many interns/associates have you personally signed off on?*
3. *Have you ever had to remediate/fire an intern/associate? Why?*
4. *Do you want me to practice a particular theory or can I explore different ones?*
5. *Can I see a sample of the paperwork you will expect from me at supervision?*
6. *How many supervisees do you have or intend to have (less is best)?*
7. *How much do you charge?*
8. *Can I see your schedule/when do you plan to offer supervision? Will this change?*
9. *Can I see a copy of your supervision contract?*
10. *Do you have emergency procedures for critical incidents with clients (are you readily available)?*

Remember, you will be with your supervisor for three thousand hours. That may take you eighteen to twenty-four months, or it may take you five years. Make sure you respect, enjoy, and feel challenged by your supervisor. A supervisor who is either all-challenge or a pushover will not give you a quality experience. Don't be afraid to admit if you have made a mistake; cut the ties and move on. Your career depends on it.

Choose the Right School

It is likely that since you are reading this book, then you are already in a master's program working on your degree. If you are not, then you must choose an adequate graduate program. Choosing your graduate school counselor education program carefully is important because that choice could impact whether or not you get hired, and whether or not you get paid.

Counselor education programs have different requirements, curricula, practicum experiences, and opportunities. Because the programs can be so different, it is wise to choose one accredited by an outside accrediting body. CACREP, (Council for Accreditation of Counseling and Related Educational Programs) is a respected accrediting body for counselor education programs. Many third-party payers (insurance companies) and employers recognize CACREP and will welcome your services. Schools without that accreditation may not give you that same benefit. For a list of CACREP accredited schools, use the Google machine and do a search in your location of choice.

CACREP is not the only way to know if a counseling school will be a good fit for you. Here are some questions to ask:

- Do your courses align with the licensing requirements for counseling in my state?
- Do you have a counseling clinic on campus where counseling students can do their supervised practicum hours?
- Do you offer a counseling doctoral program?
- How many full-time faculty do you have? How many adjunct?
- (For CACREP accredited schools) Where is the link so I can see the data you collect for CACREP?
- (For online counseling programs) How do students complete practicum hours?

Choose Your Clients Carefully

I looked at my client and noticed his posture changing. His wife had just said, to his surprise, she wasn't there because she wanted to save the marriage. She was there because she wanted to tell him in front of a third party (me) that she wanted a divorce. We were only fifteen minutes into a ninety-minute session. This was going to be a long one.

No worries though, I had helped lots of couples navigate those waters, and I felt my insecurity dissolve as I went through my next steps.

"Did you hear what Karen (not her real name) said Joe (also not his real name)?"

"I heard her," said Joe. "I just don't agree. I won't agree. She doesn't get to decide for me and she can't control me."

The session didn't get much better. Thirty minutes later:

"Joe, you can't make Karen stay married. Furthermore, I can't make Karen want to stay married to you," I said. "When two people come to counseling for their marriage, I must honor both parties and their goals for counseling."

"Can't we make this a goal for therapy?" Joe asked, "To help Karen see that she is making a huge mistake?"

"I can't give Karen a goal she doesn't want. That isn't how therapy works," I replied.

"That's unacceptable. I heard you were a good therapist. I guess I was wrong," Joe said.

Forty-five minutes to go. Karen was being awfully quiet.

With about fifteen minutes left, I stopped Joe for the third time because his voice was elevated, spit was flying from his mouth at Karen, and he was edging toward her on the couch. I made the choice to end the session and both left my office. No further appointments were requested (or recommended). Karen headed for the bathroom and Joe headed for the front door of the office.

Just another day at the office in the world of marriage counseling!

Marriage counseling can be tough, but disgruntled partners are a part of the territory. Marriage counselors are trained for that. Difficult clients and dangerous situations are another story, however. One of my favorite speakers, an attorney who has defended lots of Texas counselors, discussed how hanging on to difficult clients like Joe, can turn into a liability. Terminating a client can be hard for counselors. We don't want our client to feel abandoned, and we want to make sure there is continuous care. Most professionals recommend an ethical, decision-making model to help us make difficult decisions like this. I was considering my options regarding terminating Karen and Joe when I saw the Facebook review.

Joe had found our practice on Facebook and had written a scathing review. No big deal; we had dealt with this kind of thing before. I was able to take the comment down and prevent further posts. Then the emails started coming. We never give our personal email to clients but Joe had apparently tried every permutation of my name, common email suffixes, and my business name and had somehow landed on my personal email. His email was threatening; I was starting to get nervous. I decided to immediately take ethical action to protect myself.

In your master's degree, you probably learned about several ethical decision-making models. Gerald Corey, Ed.D. has written numerous books about this and he gives us six steps to take when we are trying to make an ethical decision:

1. *Identify the problem or the dilemma.*
2. *Identify the potential issues involved.*
3. *Review the relevant ethical codes.*
4. *Know the applicable laws and regulations.*
5. *Obtain consultation.*
6. *Consider possible and probable courses of action.*

After taking all these steps, I chose to terminate the counseling relationship with the couple. I chose to terminate via telephone and U.S. mail. First, I contacted Karen. I let her know my decision and that she would be receiving a letter in the mail offering her and Joe some referrals for both individual and couple counseling. Karen listened and told me she understood. She also volunteered that the same thing had happened with their last marriage counselor. I tried to call Joe several times and could not reach him. I did not leave a voicemail. Both letters were sent out certified mail at the same time, and I documented my decision.

Although rare, whether you are in private practice or seeing clients in an agency, scenarios like these are a part of any counselor's career. Choosing your clients carefully is important because research tells us clients like Joe can be the most litigious. Difficult clients are inevitable, but allowing them to become a liability to your career doesn't have to be.

Understand Countertransference

Another reason to choose your clients carefully is due to countertransference. New therapists often start their counseling career trying to help the population they feel closest to. New therapists who were survivors of domestic violence want to work at the women's shelter; therapists who have parented difficult teens want to teach parenting classes at their church; counselors in recovery want to work with teens struggling with addiction. Is any of this a problem?

When a new therapist works with clients who suffer because of issues they have also experienced, they can experience countertransference, which can cloud judgment and impact effectiveness with clients. Any time you feel like you are over-identifying with (or becoming attracted to) your client seek consultation in supervision, and consider referring to a colleague.[2] While over-identifying with your client can lead to difficulties, so can rejecting a client based on an internal dialogue that says, "I have strong feelings about this client's (romantic partner, culture, gender, race, etc.), so there is no way I can help her. I need to refer her for her own good." Referring a client because you have a moral objection or implicit bias is unethical. If you anticipate you may not be able to work with a certain population then you must seek out supervision for yourself. But don't do the work just to decrease your liability. Do the work to make yourself open, accepting, and affirming of all clients who will come through your door. Do it to become a better person.

What about Being in an Agency or Setting Up a Private Practice?

In chapter three, I described how I teach new counselors to visualize success. Whether they visualize an afternoon twice a week where they can be there for their kids, or a Bentley in the garage, they must decide if that avenue is through counseling in an agency or in their own private practice. Knowing the pros and cons of working in an agency or in a private practice is important because each will pose different challenges to your license. In the coming chapters I will discuss federal and state laws that pertain to practicing in both arenas; however, knowing the laws is not enough. Here are a few pros and cons I came up with for each:

---

[2] For more information on countertransference: https://www.goodtherapy.org/blog/psychpedia/countertransference

Agency:

Pro	Con
Fixed work schedule	May have to travel to several sites
Steady paycheck	Pay may be low
No marketing – clients are provided	May not be able to pick and choose clients – you get what you get
Benefits may be included	Work can be dangerous and chaotic

Private practice:

Pro	Con
Create your own schedule	May need to work afternoons or weekends
Charge what you like	Paycheck can fluctuate
You can create a niche and specialize	You must market your services
You can possibly make more money to set aside for a rainy day	No benefits – you must create own retirement and health insurance

Next Steps…

Read the following questions and answers in the next section:

The Experts Weigh In.

After their comments, write your own answers.

What are the top two mistakes you've made in your practice and how did you fix them?

Janet: *I let others handle my money. That was a big mistake. I worked at two practices early in my career where they had a receptionist who made appointments and took the money, and that was a huge mistake. The second time, the second practice that I was in, I was scared to take my own money, and it was really hard for me to ask people for their money, but I got really good at it, because I had to pay the rent, and I had to pay my overhead, and I needed to make a salary. So, I got very, very good at feeling confident about asking people to pay me for the session, and I found different ways to do that.*

The other thing that I regret and really learned is that I thought that I had to be connected with a big name. I thought that I kind of had to ride on their coattails, and I was very scared to leave a very successful practice and launch out on my own, and this was many, many, many years ago. I thought that people would not see my value if I left that particular place, and that couldn't have been anything further from the truth.

I had to really push myself to move away from that and to start my own thing, and when I did, it was just like night and day. It was a really positive thing. As much as I loved those people and miss them, it was a positive thing. It was time to move on, so don't be afraid to move on.

Cheryl: *I wrote two down, but I'm going to add a third. The first mistake is that I went into private practice right away, which I'm so thankful for. It was such a great opportunity. But because of that, I never worked in a mental health clinic, I never did any hospital work, so that's a regret of mine,* *because I feel that there's a gap in some knowledge that I'd like to learn, but once you've gotten a taste of how wonderful it is to be in private practice, sometimes it's hard to push the pause button and enter into a clinical setting or in-hospital. So that's one regret.*

The second regret is I still don't have ... I mentioned flows and systems before, I still don't have a perfect system that works for me for paperwork. I'd like to be completely paperless, and I don't quite have that yet. I haven't taken the time. So, I regret not planning that ahead of time, but I'll get to it.

Then the third one is just not attending enough trainings. I think, once you start building up practice, then you use your time to see clients, and it's hard to take a break from that.

Christopher: *We made two big mistakes. One, we started trying to file to accept Aetna insurance, and it wasn't filed correctly, and we're still dealing with that, and that started a year ago. Our group is not actually credentialed with Aetna, individual providers are, and it's a real nightmare, and Aetna has not been very helpful. That was one aspect of the insurance thing.*

The other mistake was probably accepting Magellan. Part of our model is affordable care, and so we really believe in providing reliable, professional, affordable care to clients. And I want to say yes to people, and I want them to come in and see a therapist, but Magellan's reimbursement rate is very low. That's not a big deal if Magellan clients are 1% or even 10% of our client population. But when it gets to the level that it is now, it really, really causes problems…that's one of those executive decisions that you have to try to look down the road as far as you can and say is this gonna be worth it?

And then, I did hire two people...and I wish I would have filtered that a little bit. I rectified that by firing them. It was a waste of money and time, and so I felt that maybe I wasn't clear enough about how unique our model is when they came on board. One lady thought that we were hiring her company to come work for us, her private practice. I said no, it's W2. When we issued her first paycheck, she was confused why it wasn't made out to her private practice. I told her why and that was just a nightmare.

The other one was an intern who just was not a good fit at all, and just was a big drain, and so I found another supervisor, and moved her over.

Jean: *This happened fairly recently, and I'm willing to admit this, I raised my rate without really thinking as much as I should have about when was the last time that I raised my rate. And that's always a hard one....and you get to this point where you're like, "It's my business. Unless I'm doing something legally or ethically wrong, I can (raise my rates) really."*

But I've got to figure out how I want to do this. So typically, it's recommended not to change your rate really more than once a year...and it hadn't been quite a year since I raised my rates the last time for my group. I presented it to my group and they had very interesting reactions. It turned into a really great group discussion and we've grown a lot from that.

But it was a huge learning opportunity for me, and if that would have happened in the past it would have been much more difficult for me to deal with. But I was able to make a therapeutic intervention with that and change it. It was great, but it was very difficult in that they were either overly accepting, but angry and not showing it. Or telling me, "You know I don't care what kind of certification you have now, you just raised your rates. I'm not okay with this." In a group setting and it's all coming at me, that's difficult. Part of me says, "Well, it's just the way it is. Deal with it." And it's kind of what came out, in a way.

So how I dealt with that, besides talking to my therapist, was to consult with every other therapist that I know who gave me every advice that exists on the planet from, "you can do it however you want to do it," to "what are you learning from this?" to "that's all their stuff"…and they're trying to protect me because they want to support me…because they wouldn't want me to be in that situation. The next couple of weeks I sat back down with the group and I felt like I was doing everything wrong, but my intuition was saying, "How do I keep the group more important than anything else? So how can we do this?"

I came back the next week and told them after thinking about it and considering their reactions, that this was not a good time to raise my rates. I did not feel comfortable raising it if it was creating such a reaction in everyone. I asked if we could re-evaluate my rates later. I didn't even give them a timeline. I'm waiting to do that.

And the other mistake is, kind of going back to the impulsivity of wanting it now; I have made decisions, especially regarding office locales…and not being wise, but being impulsive. Like I want it now. Thinking, 'this is a great office' and because I didn't really listen to my intuition, it just wasn't a place where I needed to be. I should have waited a little bit longer to find a space that was more conducive, but I wanted it so I could start. Now!

It's that, you know, what is it that's really going to satisfy me versus what's going to make me feel worthy right now. So how I've worked on that is, I've moved a lot of offices. And I've learned, learning to still be open, still take risks, still take chances yes, but make wiser choices. It's okay to wait a little bit. Your clients will be okay. You'll be okay. And wait for the thing that really fits.

Katherine: *So, the top mistake was becoming a Medicaid provider, and I haven't figured out how to fix it yet. I'm committed to being a Medicaid provider. I believe in providing services to the population that has the greatest need. So, I'm committed to figuring it out, I just haven't figured it out yet. And the steps that I'm taking to figure it out, how to fix this are, I keep searching for the answers to the questions or the barriers to figuring it out.*

So, when we keep being denied clients and we can't get paid, I just keep asking questions. I ask other providers who billed Medicaid, how do you make it work? I go to training on Medicaid billing and all of that, and I talk to Medicaid insurance providers. I hear what people say, people who have worked for them, and I try that, and I just keep trying. I haven't figured it out yet.

This is not a mistake, but when I saw this question, this was one of the things that popped in my head. So I waited until my son died to start my private practice, and I will never forget the conversation with him one day on the way to church. He was getting close to turning 16, and he was gonna get a church job, and him saying to me, "Mom, when are you going to start your private practice? I'm going to be working soon. I want to help you, and when are you going to do it?" And me saying to him, "Mi hijo, it's too risky. I can't do it. I'm a single mom. I have to

> *have a set job with a steady income with benefits so I can take care of you." And he's like "you've got to take more risks, we'll be okay, and you just have faith, you know?"*
>
> *I didn't take the risk when he was alive, and I don't perceive not taking the risk as a mistake. I don't perceive that. I am extremely comfortable with the decision that I made. And if I were in the situation all over again, I would probably make the same decision. But I share that to share that I do wonder, what if I had been so brave, you know what I mean?*

Kate: *My favorite mistakes of all time? Or this week? Around 2010 I fired an intern who ended up filing a complaint against me (It was thrown out for lack of merit). One year I forgot to save enough money for taxes. Then there was the time I hired a bookkeeper who took six to eight hours once a month to do my books and once she finished, would cut herself a check for eight hundred dollars. As a result of my mistakes I created excellent supervision paperwork, efficient management systems, a wonderful intern acquisition process, and the ability to confront people and stop avoiding conflict.*

Your Answers:

What are two mistakes that scared you?

1._____

_____

2._____

_____

How did you fix them?

_____

_____

_____

_____

_____

_____

_____

_____

_____

What good came from your mistakes? (you learned to ask for help, you faced your fear of confrontation, etc.)

_____

_____

_____

_____

_____

_____

_____

_____

_____

Chapter 5

THE THERAPEUTIC USE OF MONEY

Money, get away.
Get a good job with more pay and you're okay.
— **David Gilmour**

New counselors know fear is a part of success just like a cramp is a part of winning a marathon. Sadly, fear is also a part of failure. Fear-based decisions such as neglecting paperwork, DIY bookkeeping, and solo decision-making, can kill a counseling career before its third anniversary. For counselors in private practice, the fear can turn into an ethical issue. Fearful owners of a struggling young practice may start to see each client as a dollar sign rather than a relationship.

Don't get me wrong; fear **will** be your constant companion on the road to success in business. You just can't let it drive. In this chapter, I'll cover the number one tool that will help mitigate new-counselor fear and replace it with confidence. I'm talking about cold hard cash.

When I talk about money, it always makes counselors a little uneasy. Money, like time and food, can become a symbolic manifestation for other emotions like comfort, confidence, and safety. For our purposes in this chapter, I will talk about money in terms of its use as a safety net and confidence builder. I will teach you how cash can help you navigate mistakes, develop solutions that will keep your career on track, and unleash your creativity so you can grow as a counselor.

In the previous chapter I mentioned my fee-splitting mistake. It was a doozey. I have talked about this particular mistake at conferences and courses, but I rarely get into the depths of Charlie Foxtrot this particular mistake was (you non-military readers will have to Google that). Allow me to explain.

My Favorite Mistake

I invited some therapists to join achievebalance.org and in exchange for the promise of stimulating conversations, mastermind meetings, a killer brand, and group consultations, I would only charge them rent (I was the leaseholder on several offices) plus a percentage of their client fees. I call this the 'hair salon' model. I rent you a booth and take a portion of your income for my overhead. It started off well enough. I met some very nice therapists who wanted to open or grow their private practices, they signed my contract, and started paying their sub-lease rent. When they started seeing clients, I got a portion of their client fee. I was making money; they were making money; life was good.

After some time passed, I noticed a few problems.

1) Problem number one was that even though I offered regular meeting times, most of my new colleagues weren't coming to the mastermind meetings or the consultation groups. This led to problem number two.

2) I noticed that the ones who didn't make it to the meetings couldn't pay their rent.

3) The last straw (problem number three) was when one of the therapists, whom I rarely saw, received a complaint for doing something I told her not to do.

There were some bright spots in this arrangement. Before I learned what I was doing that was unethical, I made quite a bit of money. (I'll talk more about this in the "Pay Your Taxes" section). Also, I did have a couple of counselors who met regularly to consult and brainstorm. As expected, their practices began to grow, and we became good friends. These women built stellar practices and were soon able to go off on their own and form their own independent practices.

After the complaint was filed against the therapist I mentioned earlier (the one who skipped consultation), the 2014 ACA code of ethics update, and Ann Marie "Nancy" Wheeler's article "The Complex Issue of Fee Splitting" came out in the May 2014 issue of Counseling Today, I shut this part of my practice down. I still had my own clients, but I let my rented offices go and terminated the contracts with the other therapists working under me. Consequently, here's what happened…

- The therapists that did not do so well faded into the sunset.

- The stellar therapists are still doing quite well and they remain good friends, amazing referrals, and reliable referral sources.

- I brushed myself off and braced myself for the consequences of this business failure. Shutting down that arm of the practice was the right decision ethically, but it slammed me financially.

If my husband had not had a savings account set aside, it would have been a real financial hardship for my family. That wasn't the first time my supportive husband balanced the weight of my life decisions. When I made the leap from full-time teacher to full-time counseling student, and when I made the leap from fully employed counselor to private practice entrepreneur, his income supported us while I pursued my dream and got on my feet.

Build a Bridge

> **Ask yourself...**
>
> - Do I have or can I create a bridge for my counseling practice?
> - What is my main bridge, and what is my backup bridge if the main one collapses?
> - How much cash is enough to mitigate my fear?

To pursue my career in counseling, I had to focus on getting from the secure foundation I was standing on to the scary precipice I could see in the distance. Although many of my decisions seemed like "leap before you look" or "jump and the parachute will find you" decisions, in every case, I had a bridge to support my journey.

What exactly is a bridge? A bridge is the cash reserve, savings account, good budget, outside job, or income from a supportive partner that keeps you from quitting. Bridges are important because graduate school is expensive and can deplete a family's resources. Bridges are important after graduation when you are pursuing your three thousand hours because life happens. Illness, hurricanes, the flu, a sick parent, a sick child, something will eventually impact your life. A financial bridge between the startup phase of a new career and the "It's going to be okay because I'm finally making a decent living" phase is important because scarcity, even if it is perceived scarcity, creates anxiety.

When anxiety goes up, cognition goes down so your ability to do well in school, be creative in your private practice, be completely focused on your clients in your agency or private practice, will be negatively impacted if you are worried about paying your bills.

Case Study — Bob the Entrepreneur

Let's take Bob as our example.

Bob wants to be a counselor. He has a great job as a pilot but he's ready to follow his passion and help others. He knows he must secure a master's degree in counseling or a related field, an internship site for his three thousand hours, and a job. From his life experience he knows:

- Mistakes are inevitable and can be expensive.
- It takes time to study and pursue a graduate degree.
- He probably can't keep his pilot position while he puts in the hours he needs to finish his internship.
- If he chooses to work in an agency, he will probably make less money than he made as a pilot.
- If he chooses private practice, it will take time to build his income up to "pilot-level."
- He must pay his own bills and buy groceries for his family in the meantime.

This can all be scary stuff.

So, Bob is asking himself some critical questions:

"Where can I get the financial safety net so I can focus on doing a good job in grad school?"

"How can I keep the lights in my own home on until I finish my internship and get a good job?"

"What can I do besides get another credit card or bank loan in order to start my own private practice?" Easy now, Bob, you need a bridge. Where can Bob look?

1. **Enlist your supportive partner.** Bob's husband Stan has a great job in the oil and gas industry and he fully supports Bob's decision to go back to school and become a counselor. They agree that for five years Stan will carry a heavier load paying the family bills so Bob can devote time to school and building his career. Because he is less pressed to bring home an income, Bob can get good grades, choose a great supervisor for his internship, and make the decision to pursue agency or private practice based on passion not scarcity. Family and friends who believe in you are willing to invest in you.

2. **Don't quit your day job.** While Bob was going to school to get his counseling degree he worked part time in a restaurant. He was a bartender in college and those skills came right back when he needed them. In one semester of bartending one night each week he made enough to pay for the next semester's coursework. He did decide to get a student loan for one semester, but he only used part of it and was able to pay it back quickly. Once he graduated he got a job doing PRN work at a local psych hospital for his internship.

3. **Live on the feathers not the chicken.** Bob knew he would not make a lot of money at the hospital. Also, he was leaning toward opening a private practice once he finished his internship. He was aware of the cyclical nature of business from working at his airline. He and Stan sat down and looked at the family finances and created a lean-but-comfortable budget. They agreed to live off this lean budget even when Bob's practice took off and put any extra profit into a financial safety net savings account and tax savings account. Since the family's basic needs were always met, Bob didn't panic and make fear-based decisions when cash flow was down.

Pay Your Taxes

If you are planning to work for an agency, school, or hospital, you can skip this section because you will probably have taxes taken out of your salary each month. We'll see you in Chapter 6 which is about time management! Private practice owners and someday-practice-owners this section is for you.

One of my favorite mistakes I made as a new therapist was not setting aside money for taxes. I became a school teacher when I graduated from college, and before that I worked in restaurants and orchestras. I had no idea that when I started my private practice there was no cosmic central office magically making sure I was putting aside money for taxes and retirement. Remember when I described the multiple layer cake of mistake my fee-splitting arrangement created? Tax time was the bitter icing on top.

The problem with a big practice is, you may see lots of money pass through your office, but that money may or may not be all profit. When I had my "big" practice that was one bright side. I had a lot of money but not a lot of profit. The takeaway? If you are going to have your own private practice, you must always set aside money for taxes and retirement.

Income versus Profit

When you take money from your clients for counseling services, that is your income. When you write a check for rent, that is a business expense. Ideally your income will be greater than your expenses. When that happens, you have made a profit. The government taxes you on your profit.

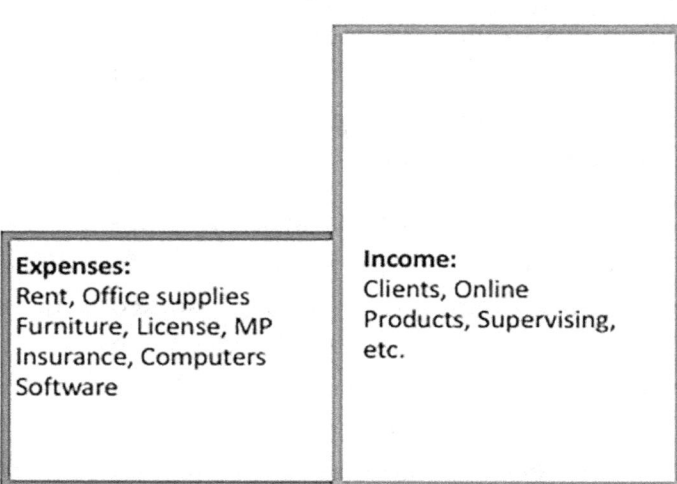

When your business makes just enough income to pay expenses, we say that it is "breaking even." There is no profit and so, you may not have any taxes to pay.

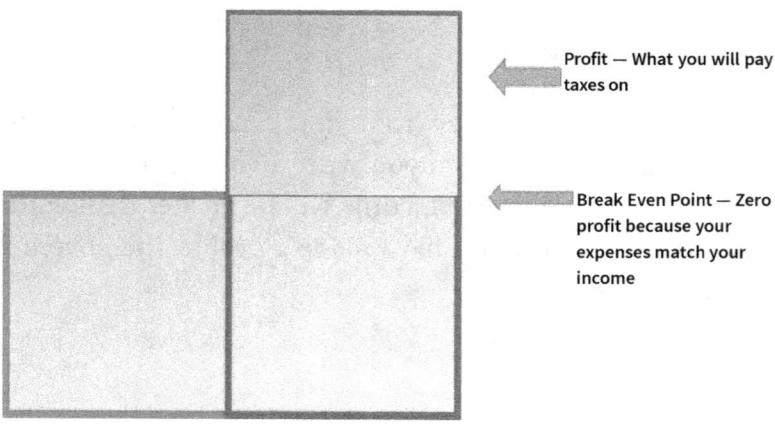

The Therapeutic Use of Money

Here's how you find your tax bracket and federal tax payments:

1. Determine your profit by subtracting your expenses from your income.

2. Google "IRS tax bracket _____ (insert year)." Lots of helpful websites will pop up including the IRS site. I found this site really helpful for figuring out my tax bracket.[3]

3. Determine your filing status (single, married, etc.). You will have the option to add your partner's profit/income if you wish.

4. Do the math based on your tax bracket.

The U.S. government has seven tax brackets. Your profit will probably fall over more than one. Here is a chart representing three of the seven tax brackets for 2017:

SINGLE 2017

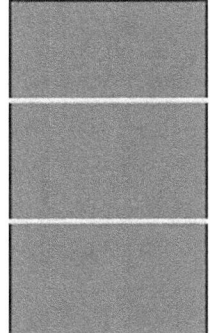

Bracket 3: $37651 - $91150 = 25%

Bracket 2: $9276 - $37650 = 15%

Bracket 1: $0 - $9275 = 10%

From the chart above you see that if you are single and your profit was $9275 or less last year then your tax bracket will be 10% and you will pay $927.50 in taxes. If you are single and your profit was $19,000, however, then we need to do a little bit of math.

---

[3] http://blog.taxact.com/how-tax-brackets-work/?utm_source=TaxACT&utm_medium=Tax-Bracket-Calculator&utm_campaign=Learn-More

According to our 'Single' chart above — you are in the 15% tax bracket. Don't pay 15% of your total $19,000 though! The tax chart is incremental. That means for our example you will pay 10% on your first $9275, then 15% on what is left over.

Here's the math:

Step 1. 10% of $9275 = $927.50 to pay in taxes. That takes care of your first bracket.

Step 2. Subtract $9275 from $19000 and you get $9725. This is the amount in the 15% tax bracket so it will be taxed at 15%.

15% of $9725 = $1458.75. That takes care of your second bracket.

Step 3. $1458.75 + $927.5 = $2386.25 is what you will pay in taxes. This is about 13% of your profit.

My shortcut? Since I don't always know my profit margin from day to day, I don't know my tax bracket. To be on the conservative side, I simply put aside about 15% - 20% of my **income** every month into a regular savings account. So, for every $100 my clients pay me, I put aside $20. When I figure out my profit margin and my tax bracket at the end of the year (remember, my profit will be lower than my income due to business expenses), I will have enough to pay my taxes AND put any extra money into a SEP IRA retirement plan. This lowers my taxes even more!

As a private practice owner, getting in the habit of setting aside money for taxes is important. If you don't have the cash at the end of the year, you might have to take out a second mortgage or put your taxes on a credit card. Refusing to pay your taxes is not an option.

What to Charge Your Clients

Confidently knowing and communicating what to charge your clients for your services is important because consistency correlates with fairness. Charging different amounts for different clients can seem discriminatory. Also charging your clients and understanding the therapeutic use of money helps your clients understand accountability and the value of your time. I'll cover this more in the section devoted to private practice in chapter eight.

 **Next Steps…**

Take a deep breath. You survived the money chapter without freaking out. Now seriously, there were some things that really informed or convicted you in this chapter. So, list the three next steps you must do immediately in order to handle money and move forward with your counseling career goals:

   1._____

   2._____

   3._____

Put a date by each one focusing on when you will take that necessary step!

Here's what the experts say about saving for retirement:

Do you have a retirement plan?

Katherine: *Yes, absolutely, 100%. I have a retirement plan through the university, but I also have a retirement plan through my practice. I was able to establish a retirement plan through my practice a couple of ways. First of all, by just* *going out and meeting with the financial advisors, and identifying, based off my situation, what that retirement plan could look like in terms of a Roth IRA and other types of individual retirement account options that we're allowed to have.*

I did that on my own, and then as my practice grew, and grew in staff size, it allowed us the ability to negotiate more retirement options, so the business now provides retirement as a benefit. Just like we provide medical, vision, and dental, we also provide retirement for team members, if they choose it.

Jean: *I have an IRA. And we do have retirement plans to move to the Seattle area.*

Christopher: *We have a traditional IRA. Whenever they say you owe $10,000 in taxes, I'm like are you sure about that? Because I could just put it over here in my IRA. We also have an investible HSA…a health savings account that we can invest up to $6,700 in a year, and what we don't use is investible. It actually acts kind of like an IRA, except you use it more regularly for medical expenses, so the investment payout is a little bit less. But when you hit a certain age, like after your kids go off to college, when they're off your plan and it's just you two, you can actually roll it into your IRA. It's like a booster shot into your IRA, when you go into your 50s. Then we also have a convertible whole life insurance policy, so that if I die now, my family is secure. When I turn 60 or 65, I can convert it into a borrowable annuity, and so it actually pays out much more.*

That's our basic retirement package, and then we have a few other assets that we're building on.

Cheryl: *My husband is the financial person in our family. I trust him. I lean on him for that.*

Janet: *I wasn't sure what you meant by that, so I'll just answer it in my own way. When I think of the word retirement, it doesn't really resonate with me, because I feel like there are so many things in the world that need to be done and that I have learned so much over the past 25 years that to me, I don't know that I'll ever retire. I'll never forget, when I was at the Appalachian Psychotherapy Conference almost four years ago now, Aaron Beck was ill, but his daughter, Judith, Skyped him in, and there were 6,000 therapists there, and so we got to hear Aaron Beck live through Skype, and he was still seeing clients, and he was still doing research, and he was 92 years old. The field of psychotherapy four years ago was just a hundred years old. He had been there almost at the inception of the field of psychology, and I was just like, "Wow, what a gift he has been," and I just loved the fact that he's still learning and he's still contributing all of his wisdom and all that he has accrued over the years with the rest of us and with his clients and with research.*

I thought, "How awesome is that?" And it really struck me, and I thought, "I may not work as much as I do right now, but I don't know that I'll ever be able to completely retire." Retirement to me sounds kind of boring. I feel like I've got to do something purposeful and useful, but it just may not be at the capacity that I'm doing now.

Kate: *I have had several retirement and savings plans through the years. My teacher retirement, or as I like to call it my small business loan, paid for opening expenses for achievebalance.org in 2007. Every time I work at a university I get a small retirement plan, or as I like to call it my* *daughter's volleyball fund, that I cash out when my position ends or I decide to take a break. In all seriousness, my husband and I each have had retirement plans for several years. His plan through the army will provide a pension, and health benefits. My SEP IRA lowers our taxes each year and will provide a monthly income when (and if) we choose to retire.*

Chapter 6

MAKE TIME

*Time, time, hear the bells chime, over the harbor and the city.
Time, one more vodka and lime to help paralyze
that tiny little tick, tick, tick, tick....*
—Christine Ellen Hynde

In 2007, I chose the name "Achieve Balance" for my counseling practice. I had just finished a PhD. My husband was back from a recent mobilization with the U.S. Army. I had completed my last reconstruction surgery following a double mastectomy, and I was starting a business. Oh, and I had three kids under the age of fifteen. Success wasn't an option unless I could also achieve balance. Achieving balance wasn't possible unless I could manage my time. That is how I began my search for strategies and ideas to help my ambition.

I am not, by nature, an organized person. In fact, I have had several (LOTS of) therapy sessions about things like my family's pet name for me as a child: "Kate the Flake" and "Late Kate." When I analyze myself through my thoroughly unfiltered, no countertransference lens, I figure I'm probably very ADD. I can remember getting my first planner in college and how I felt so accomplished when I wrote my assignments down with due dates. As a school teacher, the planner lost its luster as I realized I had to complete lesson plans for EVERY DAY of my school life. Pretty soon I was winging it again. Lucky for me after my second-year teaching general music in elementary school, I secured a job as an orchestra teacher. So, no more lesson plans; I just had to teach the songs and play the concert.

> **Ask yourself...**
> - Who and what are the top five time-wasters in my daily schedule?
> - How much time do I spend on average in daily self-care?
> - See #2 on list. How many 20-minute job sets will I start doing now each day?
> - What are three things on my to-do list I could do right now?

Twenty-four years, three kids, two graduate degrees, and countless trips through the Google jungle later, I have quite a few "Top 10 Strategies" and "Easy Life Hacks" that I have utilized to manage my daily schedule, weekly schedule, and yearly schedule. As a practicing counselor your daily schedule is important because counseling requires your 100 percent emotional engagement along with pristine paperwork execution. Take note of these realities:

- Sacrificing emotional engagement will negatively affect your clients.

- Sacrificing the quality of your administrative work will lead to mistakes and litigation.

- Sacrificing boundaries in order to get things done will lead to relationship difficulties with your significant others.

Your weekly schedule is important because life change happens. Kids grow up, your health changes, your ability to work eight hours each day five days each week will eventually come to an end. To make sure you are adapting, you must develop life-stage goals. These five and ten-year goals won't develop if you don't have a day to work on them each week. Likewise, your self-care won't happen if you don't schedule it each week.

Finally, but possibly most importantly is your yearly schedule. Your yearly schedule is important because that is where you will create lasting patterns of self-care, growth opportunities, relationship care, and future thinking. Perhaps you will take a sabbatical once each quarter to emotionally re-group, work on your five-year career plan, or write your novel. If you are in a relationship or have a family, you might plan a month-long vacation during the dog-days of summer when your schedule is slow. Your private practice might benefit from a yearly dinner where everyone can meet and socialize, or a yearly HIPAA training and policy and procedures review.

In this chapter, I will describe a few tactics that have been especially helpful to me over the years to win the battle over control of my calendar. Since I'm a strategic family therapist preferring to focus on what I can do rather than what I must stop, I took some of the most practical advice and 're-framed' it.

1. Original advice: **Let go of perfectionism.**

   Kate's re-frame: ***Put out the first draft and let the audience co-create.***

   I can think of VERY few successful things I have created, developed, presented, implemented, or sold, that I felt were completely 100 percent perfect. Seeing everything as a first draft allowed me to produce my art and see my audience as collaborators. The result? I have some pretty cool products and some very amazing fans.

2. Original advice: **Limit time-wasting activities and people.**

Kate's re-frame: ***Do five 20-minute job sets every day***. This is a game I play with myself using my phone timer (it's also called Parkinson's law of productivity). I set a twenty-minute timer and race the clock to see how much I can get done. I rarely finish all five sets but my productivity skyrockets when I self-impose these "deadlines."

3. Original advice: **Re-structure your life.** (What does that even mean?)

    Kate's re-frame: ***Buy back your life***. A few things I have hired out: house cleaning, grocery shopping, meal delivery, cat litter delivery, toilet paper (all kinds of personal paper) delivery, driver's ed., driving my kids, cooking, social media posting, SEO optimization, bookkeeping, accounting, and legal defending just to name a few. I want to try hiring an Uber once each week just to see what I can get done on my commute (I bet it is worth the $6.00 fare).

4. Original advice: **Manage your time.**

    Kate's re-frame: ***Clock out.*** Literally set an end time for your work every day. If you need to purchase an actual time/card punch to set on your counter, head to the Amazon machine and buy one.

5. Original advice: **Manage your calendar.**

    Kate's re-frame: ***Make some friends***. Did you know there are some people who stay busy with work because they are bored? These folks may be shy, introverted, scared, or socially anxious. They choose to be out of balance because it is easier than facing their issues. Surrounding myself with amazing friends and being an amazing friend have been two of my goals in 2017.

6. Original advice: **Purge or detox from negative, draining thoughts about yourself and others.**

   Kate's re-frame: ***Recharge by being positive and kind to yourself and others.*** Encourage yourself and hang with people who are encouragers not discouragers. Move up in every area of your life. U.S. Ambassador Dr. Suzan Johnson Cook (Dr. Su-J) wrote a great book titled, *Moving Up*. Get away from people and thoughts that are downers. Dr. Su-J writes, "Stand up; Speak up; Look up; Book up; Kiss up; Listen up; Hang up; Make up; Wake up; and Cheer up." Another way to approach this is to distance yourself from friends and colleagues who are moving down; associate with those who are *moving up*.

Plan, take control of, and use your time wisely, it's really the only currency you own and have complete control over…if you choose.

 **Next Steps…**

Review the six advice statements you just read which were re-framed by Kate. Which one do you need the most? Re-frame it in your own words and describe how you will implement it:

_____

_____

_____

_____

_____

Here's what the experts say about schedules:

What is one thing you wish you could change about your daily schedule?

Cheryl: *Daily, I wish that I could get up about an hour earlier than my kids so that I just have some quiet time. And I guess I probably could, but I just don't, so I hit the snooze button way too often.*

Christopher: *I think my daily schedule is kind of in a really good spot right now.*

Jean: *I would like to be more consistent, more certain of what my day is going to look like. And that's hard because when you have maybe a couple of clients that cancel and you have a couple of hours, you're like, "What am I going to do with those hours?" And I know we've talked about that in many different realms of what do you do with that time. I'm not always consistent with using that time well. I think, "What am I going to do with myself? What do I do?" Some days I will unconsciously not bring something to do, so I end up wasting that time or I feel anxious in those moments.*

Katherine: *I wish I didn't have to respond to email on a daily basis because it takes up so much time. Some of the emails take a lot of thought. They take a lot of time drafting a response, and that's mentally draining, and it takes away from the energy that it takes to run a business, and interact with people, like really interact with them versus interact with them via the email. It takes up a lot of time because then I find I'm in conversations back and forth over email, back and forth, back and forth, back and forth versus just responding to email and being done with it, and moving* on. *It's just like an ongoing conversation, and I get the sense that people expect a quick response via email. And so, if I could not respond to email on a daily basis, if I could just bank all those emails, and respond to them on one day of the week, where that's all I did was just do email all one day of the week and not have to touch it the rest of the time, man, that would just be awesome. That would just be really great.*

Janet: *I've been a counselor of some sort for 25 years. I started out as an LCDC back in 1989, and then eventually I went back to graduate school to get my LPC, so I've been doing this for a few years now. What I'd really like to do is work at my office three days a week and do one whole day of equine, and I'd like to be home because I do my equine business on my property.*

Kate: *I don't like my tendency to grab my computer and work on random things throughout the day. For example, if I have thirty minutes between clients, or an hour before my daughter gets home from school, or three hours by myself before bed, I will pull out my computer and tweak my website or polish my writing. As a remedy I always have a new book for enjoyment on my Kindle or cued up in my Audible.*

What would you change about your weekly schedule?

Cheryl: *Weekly, things are pretty good right now. What I used to wish I could change is, I wished I could work fewer evenings, so I did change that. I went from working Tuesday, Thursday, to Tuesday, Wednesday, and now I have five days in a row to be with the family. Previously, I felt stuck in it because it was a routine that we had for about a year and a half, and then we realized that we could change* *that. Just make a few tweaks, and it's been wonderful so far. We're only two weeks into the new schedule, but so far, so good.*

Christopher: *I have Fridays as an administrative day that I can work from home. And then, I have Saturdays and Sundays off. I only see about eight to twelve clients a week. And then, I get to teach the classes that I want to teach at the time spots that I want to teach usually...so that's been really good, and then to have enough time to manage and spend time with my staff is good. I took on a course this summer to teach in Houston on Mondays, so it was an all-day thing. I'd actually fly down in the morning, teach a class, and fly back at night.*

I did that for 12 weeks in a row, and that just ended two weeks ago. But I decided ... because that ended, that I wasn't going to tell anybody, and so I told my staff just to assume that I'm still in Houston. Now I have this whole new day where I go in the office and I just sit at my desk for eight hours and work, ... the last two weeks have been extremely productive doing that.

Jean: *My answer is to try to be more consistent and less variable. Because my practice in The Woodlands is pretty full, I have very little time. I have two days in The Woodlands, two days in my Houston office. And I'm building in my Houston office, so that's where I see a lot of the empty chunks of time. And in my Woodlands office, I'm back to back. Sometimes no lunch... it feels like all or nothing. And yet the offices are on opposite days. So I kind of feel that I don't know how that is affecting me... are my practices doing okay, or not? And trying to build in one location but trying to keep the other balanced and not overload it...I'm trying to figure that out.*

Katherine: *The one thing I would change about the weekly schedule is I just wish I worked less. I work a lot, and so it would be nice to have more time off. I am an assistant professor and I won two very large federal grant projects. I have a very full schedule. I basically have two full-time jobs. I run a practice…a business, and I have my full-time job with the university. Both of those jobs are more than 40-hour-a-week jobs, so I do work every day just to maintain a minimal level of performance.*

Kate: *I feel like Cheryl; if I have a problem with my schedule I change it. Private practice is cyclical in nature so if I know I will be taking time off for a vacation or I know it's the time of year my clients tend to drop off, I will open up my week and try to see as many as twenty clients. If it is volleyball season or I want to visit my kiddo at school or work, then I have the flexibility to open up my schedule and do that. I love that about being in private practice.*

What would you change about your yearly schedule?

Cheryl: *I love time off with my kids, and they go to public school, the older ones do, and I would love if summers were longer and we just had more family time or down time, time to hang out. I take off some time. I make the hours look a little bit different, but I think it's just nice having everybody home under the same roof and more relaxed.*

Christopher: *I'd love to have a spot where I could take a month or two off, and go somewhere, or write, or just hang out. I don't think we're anywhere near that, but that would be something I would like to see. For example, it would be nice to go to the south of France, every summer, for like two or three months, and everyone knows ahead of time. I could work from there, but not see clients, not be in the* *office, focus on a special project like a book, or articles, or research, or something, or just relax.*

Jean: *It is unpredictable. I hear other therapists say, "Oh this summer's been great." And I'm like, "Well, great for you." You know it sucked for me. But then, it's like, "What am I going to do with my down time?" I don't have enough time to train. Do I do training? Should I read? So just feeling that trust, even though I've been in private practice now for quite some time, it's really just, as I'm growing, to see that there are ebbs and flows in this kind of business. You know, but what do you want to do with that time, then? And sometimes that's hard to know what you want to do. I just want the next client. That's what I want. And sometimes that's not happening.*

Katherine: *I have some pockets built into my yearly schedule, where I put on the calendar, "take vacation," but it inevitably never works out, where I can just take a vacation. For example, you and I are doing this interview, I'm away at a conference (in Orlando). The conference, although work, should've been a time where I could unplug and just learn, and have real professional development time, which for me is enjoyable, so that would be part of my wellness. But I had to take time away from the conference because something with work came up that was extremely time-sensitive. I literally had to, as soon as I could, leave the conference, and have lunch in my room. I couldn't have lunch and network with the conference, and I had to miss the next session, so I didn't get the professional development just because there was something for work that had to absolutely get done.*

So it would be nice in terms of my yearly schedule if during these pockets of time where I'm supposed to be able to take care of myself, whether that's professionally or personally, I could truly do that. If something pressing came up, it would be nice if someone else could take care of that.

And unfortunately, there are certain things in my life where there's no one else that can take care of it. If I don't do it, it won't get done, and other people are impacted if that happens.

Janet: *Yearly, what I really want to work towards is taking a month or two off. I'd like to do a month or two sabbatical. I think that'd be really invigorating, and I think it would really be a positive thing to do.*

Kate: *My yearly schedule will include a weekend away once per quarter to rejuvenate and write. I would also like to take pilgrimages to beautiful places and hike and climb. This is my goal for 2018.*

Chapter 7

ACHIEVE BALANCE

*Very early in the morning, while it was still dark,
Jesus got up, left the house and went off to a solitary place,
where he prayed.*
— Mark 1:35

I'd like you to imagine an adorable two-year old. Now imagine that two-year old poking your arm because she wants a cookie. You think to yourself, "It's not so bad, she'll stop soon," or I'm sure her parents are around here somewhere and will come get her." The poking goes on. It goes on for the rest of the day. Then it lasts weeks. Weeks turn into years.

Ridiculous, isn't it? Most of us would manage the little darling's behavior right away. Whether she got a cookie or a time out, I bet you wouldn't just ignore her and allow her to keep poking you. Stress, like the terrible twos, can't just be ignored. When you don't take an active role in managing your stress, the hormones secreted in conjunction with the stress reaction never really subside. While the exact link between stress and illness isn't always clear, we can say with confidence that stress is a factor in many common illnesses.

What is the impact on a body? The first symptoms you might notice are the physical symptoms. You experience stomach aches, your shoulders are tight, or you have migraine headaches. Perhaps you're tired all the time, have trouble sleeping, your appetite changes, or you're just not as active as you used to be. You might even have unexplained pain.

Whether you are "marrying someone or burying someone" your body interprets any change as stress and anxiety. We can never eliminate stress, but we can learn to cope with it if it's unavoidable. There are also some stressors we can learn to avoid like toxic relationships and unhealthy work environments. If you are having trouble coping with or eliminating stress from your life and you are already noticing the physical and emotional changes, this chapter is for you.

As a counselor, you can't afford to let stress get the best of you. You must practice self-care. As a counselor, self-care is important because you must be one hundred percent emotionally engaged with your clients. This by itself is taxing, because you will also have a life outside of the counseling room, you must reckon with the normal anxiety and stress due to life, family, kids, your dog, and your neighbors. To combat and cope with stress and anxiety, you must devote time and energy to discovering your own needs and triggers. Once you do this you will be able practice your coping skills before you enter the counseling room with your client.

When Anxiety Goes Up, Cognition Goes Down

When you think, you probably had a feeling first. For example, "I think I'll get a hamburger," was probably preceded by a feeling of hunger. "I think you are a jerk!" was probably preceded by a feeling of anger. The brain is always sensing and feeling and it doesn't know the difference between physical pain and emotional pain. Pain in any form demands attention when it activates the autonomic nervous system (fight or flight). In fact, it demands so much attention, that it inhibits higher level functions like logic and empathy. I'll put it this way; If I were to kick you in the knee, it would be very hard for you to feed the homeless, connect with your spouse, or do a fifth-grade math problem.

We see these types of reactions often in marriage counseling. One partner is so lonely she cannot empathize with her partner's struggles at work. The other partner is so angry at his boss he cannot co-create solutions with his wife to common parenting problems at home. The cycle is predictable:

- Both partners are in emotional pain so they are self-centered.

- Neither can connect emotionally so they distance emotionally or become passive aggressive.

- Neither can problem solve because their only goal is to sooth their own pain so they leave the room or the relationship to avoid the pain.

Basically, both physical and emotional pain make you greedy, anti-social, and stupid.

And…that's just the beginning. Physical and emotional pain not only demand attention, they direct it. Have you ever started a long drive down an interstate highway on an empty stomach? Suddenly, even if you are a vegetarian, all you notice on that long, boring drive are McDonald's and Church's chicken. You may hold out for a healthy restaurant sign, but you'll be tired and cranky when you get there.

The fact is, when you have stress, emotional pain, or anxiety, the world is either going to seem like salt or morphine. Your spouse? She better be in a good mood when you get home. Your kids? They better be behaved and have their teeth brushed. Your clients? Well they better....and that's the problem. A counselor who doesn't recognize the signs of her own emotional distress and anxiety may experience countertransference that negatively impacts her ability to help. We call that burnout. If you are already a counselor, ask yourself the following:

1. *Do you avoid thinking about your own problems and focus on others?*

2. *Do you feel bad when your clients suffer a setback or don't complete treatment?*

3. *Do you ever think about clients outside of session? These don't have to be inappropriate thoughts, but they may be intrusive and don't belong in your home.*

4. *Have you ever taken your anger/sadness out on your family members and friends? Or do you isolate to avoid interacting at all?*

5. *Do you tell yourself that counseling "takes too much out of you" during the day and you need to be alone most of the time at home to "re-energize?"*

If you agreed with a couple of the above statements, then you are probably a normal counselor. If you agreed with several, you may be teetering on the edge of burnout. It's time to get a life—a life outside of your office.

A life outside the office is important because counseling can be isolating. Some of the biggest obstacles to "life on the outside" are a natural inclination to anxiety and introversion. If you are an introvert, finding hobbies and new friends takes time and a trip outside your comfort zone. If you are inclined to anxiety, you may need to look at some blind spots and the areas in yourself you are neglecting. Either way, you have some personal self-discovery in your future. The following list may help:

- You may want to take some time and brush up on Melody Beatty's *Co-Dependent No-More* and *The Co-Dependent's Guide to the 12 Steps*.

- Assess your habits (drinking, smoking, exercising). According to the Google machine more than two drinks per night is considered heavy. So is exercising more than twenty hours per week, food restricting in the name of "clean eating," smoking a pack a day, etc. You get the idea. If you don't, you may have some blind spots.

- Ask a good friend you trust to offer feedback. Believe their feedback and do something about it.

Remember, understanding the impact of good stress and bad stress is important because your work with your clients, your family life, and your health will all be impacted. Your body doesn't care if you are marrying someone or burying someone. Both types of stress will affect your health and your work

HP and Planning for Pain

I choose to believe there is a Higher Power. Some, as in Alcoholics Anonymous©, simply refer to this power as "Higher Power" (HP) while others give the power a name like God, Allah, Universe, or Spirit. Now, here's the thing. If you have a HP, then I believe you can take everything you are worried about (and I mean *everything*), give it to this HP, and your life will improve. In fact, I believe that if you feel like you can't give everything up, then your HP is not much of a higher power and I suggest you choose a new one. Why? Because part of your plan to achieve balance as a counselor must include planning for unpleasant things in life.

Planning for pain is important because change is the only constant in life. Planning for what can go wrong without becoming negative or maintaining a negative attitude takes work. Understanding life happens, kids grow, and parents die, is important because your emotional state will affect your job and your practice. There will be a season to grieve and you must be prepared for self-care.

> **Ask yourself...**
>
> - Who is in charge of my life?
> - Who is in control of the lives of my family members?
> - If I don't remind, make lists, nag, or worry about others what will happen?
> - What are three things I could let go of easily?
> - What is one thing I tell myself I could never let go of?

Grief and grieving can be cumbersome. This is a personal story of my own journey through a small part of grief. My learning curve is still quite steep; but so far, I have learned that heavy, cumbersome grief can manifest as complete deconstruction, life change, and breakdown.

It began when my father passed away in May of 2015 at age 74 after a long illness. I cried and I thought I grieved rather well (after all, I'm a therapist). My work continued; summer dragged on; and in September, after a drawn-out probate process, we finally got the go-ahead to sell Dad's house. I think that's where things got complicated.

Over the span of about a week, my husband, daughters, and I completely emptied my parents' 3600 square-foot house. My brothers and I never lived there so it was our "grown up" home. It's where my toddlers danced in the kitchen with my mom, where I planned my "big fat Irish wedding," and where all of the sibling families gathered and celebrated holidays. Of course, I was sentimental, but that quickly turned to overwhelmed as I discovered my mom had taken "family historian" to a whole new level.

When I say that, I mean, if there were Olympic events like "Christmas Card Keeping," or "High School Scrapbook Creating," my mom would have been a gold medalist. Not only was I sorting through three sets of formal china, I found myself opening cabinets and drawers full of such treasures as: a spiral notebook with my bored doodles of Bob Seger from a 1984 chemistry class; a box with my younger brother's first lost tooth (he's 45 years old); and yellowed notes to my older brother from his high school sweethearts.

What stopped me in my tracks, though, was the discovery of my parents' wedding cake topper and my mom's diaries. The older diaries and the cake topper reflected my parents' halcyon days of babies and bridge parties. In stark contrast, the newer diaries chronicled my mom's ten-year decent into the hellish dementia of her *frontotemerolobe* (FTD) disease and her utter confusion in the face of my dad's alcoholism. Heavy stuff. Cumbersome stuff.

Like good soldiers, my husband, daughters, and I continued to clean, pack, and purge. High on our success as movers and reeling from the falling oil and gas prices in October of 2015, we impulsively made the decision to sell our own house. We moved our things to a second storage unit, our dog and cats to animal crates, and for 90 days, we kept our house meticulously clean while strangers traipsed through offering "Rotten Tomatoes-esque" reviews. In January 2016, after the last signature dried finalizing the sale of my parents' house, my husband and I mercifully removed our own house from the dying market and returned our home to order.

Heavy stuff. Cumbersome stuff…once again.

A few months after the dust settled, I sat with a friend trying to sort out what the heck had just happened. She helped me see that while I thought I was de-cluttering and dismantling two lives, in reality, I was grieving the loss of my dad, my mom, and the fact my daughter was leaving for college in the fall. In other words, life was changing, and I wasn't ready.

By fall of 2016, my house looked amazing, we were down to just one storage unit, and I helped my daughter move into her freshman dorm. Heavy and cumbersome questions remained though: Was I still a daughter? How much longer was I going to be a mom? What happens next with Dave and me? Should I sort and catalogue my Christmas cards? No, all of my existential thoughts were not tied up in a tidy bow. It's taken time (and therapy) but I believe my HP has taken me through the grieving I need to do and I'm not running away (or packing up any houses) any more.

The Reality of Compassion Fatigue

What business am I in? I am in the business of relieving pain.

I relieve my client's pain by:

- Serving them quickly – they can see me the same week they call or talk to me in most cases, the same day.

- Giving them a plan.

- Providing expert service – I am always getting CEUs and training.

- Taking care of myself so I can be 100 percent emotionally present.

If I take my job and my obligation to my clients seriously then I must learn to become an advocate for myself. If you are going to take your job and your obligation to your clients seriously you must learn to become knowledgeable about your blind spots, be aware of your family life cycle, and advocate for your own emotional health.

If you are experiencing the symptoms of compassion fatigue, get help! In Beverly Kyer's *Surviving Compassion Fatigue: Help for Those Who Help Others,* she writes, "Treatment for compassion fatigue needs to come on a variety of fronts: via supervision, employee assistance programs (EAP), team support, stress management methods, a licensed clinician, accountability partners, and one's own support community. It is only by attacking fatigue on these various fronts can the sufferers personal well-being, performance, and job satisfaction be restored." (p.172). If you need to assess the intensity and seriousness of your compassion fatigue, I recommend Kyer's book as a valuable resource for your self-care.[4]

Burnout and compassion fatigue are real and if you or I succumb, then we have robbed the world of help. Understanding the reality of compassion fatigue and weaving self-care into every day is important because if you do not, it may catch you by surprise. With physical pain we grab an aspirin or see a doctor. For emotional pain, however, we will usually cope by practicing our favorite healthy or non-healthy coping activities. No one cares how you cope on a deserted island. How you cope as a counselor affects everything and all your relationships in counseling and beyond.

 **Next Steps…**

Think of two things that you feel like only you can do, or that you absolutely can't let go of. Now take a second and close your eyes and imagine your HP taking care if it for you, without your help. Write your feelings below.

_____

_____

_____

_____

_____

---

[4] Kyer, Beverly Diane. *Surviving Compassion Fatigue: Help for Those Who Help Others* Columbus, Ohio: Gatekeeper Press (2016)

Here's what our experts say:

What is a hobby you do that has nothing to do, or very little to do with counseling?

Janet: *I love to paint. I started taking art lessons when I was twelve, so that is something that I am passionate about. I can stay very present when I'm doing that. I really did stretch a few years ago, because we have a famous artist in the little community where I live. I was able to take some classes from her. One of the things that she is very good at painting is horses, and I've never painted animals. They are very difficult to paint, and so I've been able to take some clinics from her. I got my first horse painting done a few years ago. That has been a real gift to be able to do some classes with her.*

I also treated myself a year ago and hired a horse trainer, who specializes in what we call natural horsemanship. I've never taken horseback riding lessons, and I decided to up my game in horse psychology because horses are the most amazing and interesting creatures. The experience has been mind-blowing and so exciting.

I've had plenty of training for my equine assisted psychotherapy business, and team-building business, but I've never actually taken lessons just for my own personal enjoyment and my own personal learning.

Cheryl: *I love to travel. I love going anywhere. It can be somewhere local or it can be far away, and it doesn't have to be related to what I do. We load everybody up, and that includes my husband and three boys. We go to local places or do camping or little things. We try to go somewhere big at least twice a year.*

And then I love to buy gifts for people. I know that sounds like a silly hobby, but I love ... Absolutely my love language, and if I could buy gifts for people and leave notes for people and mints on pillows, I would do that all day.

Jean: *There are two things that I pride myself in. I like to do paint by number, so I have a lot of those. As soon as I do them, I throw them away. They really mean nothing to me, just pure pleasure. And the other one is, I'm pretty good at Guitar Hero. I'm a 45-year-old therapist…and I play Guitar Hero in my down time. Those two things I do just for fun; they are not performance based.*

Chrisopher: *I love to fly fish. I go fly fishing twice a year, usually in Oklahoma, in Broken Bow, and I go up there with some of my buddies, and we disconnect. And I think my favorite thing about fly fishing is that you don't have your phone on you. You stand on the river so you don't really want to have a cell phone on you, or anything, and I also recently have stopped wearing a watch when I go, so it's a very kind of timeless experience. It's a really good way to disconnect.*

Katherine: *Yoga is my saving grace.*

Kate: *I enjoy lots of things that heal my mind and emotions. When the kids were little we loved to camp. Up until a couple of years ago I played bass for a few bands in Houston. Slowly that became something that felt like more work than play, so I cut back on it. I still enjoy playing music though. Another thing I enjoy doing is going to Austin, renting a hotel with the kids, my husband, all of the above, or all alone, and just play tourist. I adopted Austin as my home away from home after I graduated from UT in 1989. I have lived there, taught there, and visited there for almost* *thirty years and it is still my favorite getaway. And they have an amazing tattoo artist that helped me decorate my mastectomy scars with original artwork (Chris Gunn at Southside Tattoo). That's another non-guilty pleasure my husband and I enjoy. Some people buy clothes or cars; we buy ink.*

Do you meditate? How often and how long?

Cheryl: *I do. I pray. I try to pray all day long, just in little chunks. I like to break it down into thankfulness, acknowledging that God is a provider. I just ask for His wisdom and what to do next. It doesn't look like being in a room with the candles lit. It's just kind of every day walking from Starbucks to here being thankful that our paths crossed or that we get to meet or that it's so nice outside. It's kind of a daily practice, just all the time, having an attitude of gratefulness and realizing that my gratefulness comes from what God has provided for me and my family.*

Christopher: *I don't think I meditate in like the yoga sense of the word meditate…I definitely do a lot of deep thought, while journaling or just kind of sitting on my back patio just reflecting on the day. I don't sit on the yoga mat and do the "oms" kind of meditation, but I definitely reflect on the day, and think about our goals, and where we're trying to go, personally and professionally, and what worked, and what didn't work.*

Katherine: *Yes, at least three days a week. I'd say every day of the week for a small period of time, but at least three days a week for a good 45 minutes, on those three days a week, for sure.*

Jean: *Yes. Almost daily. Doing it more and more all the time. It's hard for me. I want to do yoga and meditate, I want to be active and meditate, but to just sit and meditate on something is difficult. I find myself wanting to run a lot and move, so I'm recognizing how powerful and how important it is to not do that. And how difficult it is not to do that. And yet how important it is for us to get in touch with who we are inside, not just what's going on outside.*

Janet: *I do mediate 15 minutes in the morning. I have a time of prayer, meditation, so at least 15 minutes. If I can get 30 minutes in, I do.*

Kate: *I have a morning routine where I read a devotional and memorize a verse that involves a promise. I sometimes add a reading from More Language of Letting Go by Melody Beatty. I play music called "Reiki Zen Meditation Music: 1 Hour Healing Music, Positive Motivating Energy," from YouTube https://www.youtube.com/watch?v=ye8C-F8A7r_4. I try to do 10 – 15 minutes of meditating on what I just read and memorized, as well as mindfulness. Sometimes I will take the promise I memorized and put it on a post-it note on my car steering wheel or over the RPM meter on my Jeep instrument panel (why do we need to know RPMs anyway?).*

Chapter 8

PRIVATE PRACTICE PRIMER

I keep my nose on the grindstone, I work hard every day.
Might get a little tired on the weekend, after I draw my pay.
But I'll go back workin', come Monday morning
I'm right back with the crew.
I'll drink a little beer that evening,
sing a little bit of these working man blues.
– Merle Ronald Haggard

No matter how many presentations I give on licensure laws, codes of ethics, and best practices, most audiences ask questions about private practice and becoming an entrepreneur. I'm often asked, "What is the best way to run a counseling practice?" or "What do you recommend I do first?"

The answer is complicated. In fact, one chapter won't really do the topic justice, but I'm going to try.

I started my entrepreneurial career in Junior High. There wasn't much work for a sixteen-year old in Midland, Michigan back in 1982 except babysitting. I hated it, but I could make $5 for five hours. Not bad.

My mom had put me in piano lessons when I was five and I was pretty good by the time I was sixteen, but I was getting bored. I don't remember exactly how I put two and two together, but somehow I got the idea to make some flyers and advertise thirty-minute piano lessons for little kids for $5. I would drive to their house, take them through the lesson, and thirty minutes later, I was back in my car with $5 in my pocket. I was making ten times what I made babysitting and I was actually having fun! I remember feeling a rush of freedom; I was limited only by the number of lessons I could fit into a day. I decided to fill my schedule.

My junior year, I auditioned for a local orchestra and made the bass section. I was officially a professional musician at age seventeen and making way more than I was making working the drive-through at Hardees. One rehearsal a week, one performance every couple of months. My cheerleader coach wasn't too happy. In fact, she kicked me off the team because I missed too many games. I ended up getting a music scholarship to The University of Texas though, so I got over it.

When I went to college, I took regular jobs like waitress at Red River Café and cashier at Bevo's Bookstore on the Drag, but I never stopped freelancing. I realized quickly I could work twenty hours and make $100 in one week at the book store, or I could make $300 in two days by traveling with my double bass to College Station for two rehearsals and a performance with the Brazos Valley Symphony. Or, I could make $600 for three nights with the Shrine Circus when it came to town. I took gigs playing in the pit in local musicals and as a fill-in in the UT Pep band at basketball games. I still remember walking into the mall and purchasing my first pair of expensive jeans. It was the '80s and for those of you who don't remember, jeans were a thing. I think I bought a pair of purple Jordache jeans (Google it Millennials). I was so proud of myself. Once again, even my young twenty-something brain realized I was limited only by the number of hours I was willing to practice and perform. So I practiced three – four hours every day in my little 8'x'8 practice room, and I studied, and I performed. I performed a LOT.

When I finished my degree, I began teaching elementary school general music. My work ethic was the same as it was in college so I worked hard. I remember facing every day like I was giving six little performances with a break for lunch. I loved my job and the paycheck that came with it. In my second year, I moved to Euless, Texas and in addition to my teaching duties I was asked to start a strings program after school for a little extra stipend. I moved up to a real orchestra job the year after that and taught at a middle school and high school in Richardson, Texas. I played in the local symphony in my spare time. I was a twenty-three-year old newlywed; I loved my job and my students, but I was starting to hate my paychecks. And I was getting tired.

I was working, I was teaching, and I was earning, but I felt like Lucy and Ethel on the candy conveyer belt. Not only that, kids were cycling through my classroom in one-hour increments and I was barely getting to know them. One day, I noticed my viola player was missing. I asked the kids where he was and they informed me administration had found a gun in his duffle bag, and he wasn't coming back. That completely shocked me. I was working my butt off, however, I barely knew the kids I was supposed to be teaching. To make matters worse my paycheck was barely making ends meet. I wanted to change but I didn't know how.

My first husband and I divorced shortly after we moved back to Austin in 1993. I was an orchestra teacher at a local middle school, a conductor in the after-school youth orchestra, and a single mom. After my second failed attempt at a housemate situation (I could write a book about that), my two-year old son and I moved to a new development near Houston called The Woodlands, to teach orchestra and be closer to my mom and dad. Long story short, I met my husband, Dave, soon after, and we had a beautiful baby girl in the Spring of 1998. The summer after her birth, I finally decided to take a year off.

It wasn't exactly "off" however. I taught string lessons out of my home, began training for a triathlon, and started a master's degree in counseling. Why counseling? A couple of reasons. First, my first marriage ended horrendously. A wonderful counselor helped me through it and I knew I wanted to pay it forward. Second, my own child was starting to have difficulty and it reminded me of all the kids I never connected with in my orchestras. For years I watched hundreds of kids herd in and out of my classroom, never knowing if they were sad, if I was helping, if they loved the violin, or if they were packing a gun. Now my own child was struggling in Kindergarten. It was too much; I had to slow down and help.

I decided I wanted to start a counseling private practice. So, when my baby was napping, I was studying. When school got out, I would put my son in front of the TV with a bowl of cereal and teach lessons for two hours. My husband would come home, I'd cook dinner, maybe teach a couple of lessons, then call it a day. In 1999 I went back into teaching orchestra at a middle school, and in 2000 I graduated from Sam Houston State University with my MA in counseling.

I would love to say after graduating I pursued my dream of owning my own private practice, but I was a chicken. I was scared to make the leap into counseling of any kind. My degree was only a thirty-six-hour master's degree so I wasn't even eligible to start my hours (that was back when you finished your internship hours BEFORE you took your exam). In 2002, after my husband returned from his thirteen-month mobilization and the birth of my third child, I decided to go back to school and pick up my licensing hours and start my internship. For a solid year I would teach orchestra all day and then, three nights a week I would counsel domestic violence clients at the Women's Center.

Finally in 2004, after my husband took a mobilization to Iraq, I made the leap and started counseling (he told me "it will keep you busy." Understatement of the year.). As a Licensed Marriage and Family Therapist Associate I started a small private practice in an unheated room above a bar in downtown Conroe. I taught orchestra full time, saw three to five clients each week, and if I made enough to pay my $250 rent each month, I was happy.

Well, I should probably say, happy-ish. I started my PhD in 2004, and in the spring of 2005 I got my breast cancer diagnosis. Again, it was too much for me. I closed the practice and quit my teaching job. My husband came home for the mastectomy and reconstruction surgeries and I just tried to focus on raising my family, getting healthy, and finishing school. In 2007 I graduated with my PhD in Counselor Education and re-opened my practice under a new name: achievebalance.org.

My mentor Dr. Judy DeTrude invited me to join her and I was completely energized by her guidance, and her focus on continuing education. In 2010, after the death of my mother the year before, I opened a Texas non-profit called Ann's Place to train interns and offer low-cost community counseling. When Judy retired in 2015, I rebranded the continuing education arm of our business as Kate Walker Training and continued to offer supervisor training, online courses, and counselor resources.

So, when people ask me how to run a private practice I often just shake my head. I have only run **my** practice. It's been a wild ride and I have done the best I could to increase my skills, operate ethically, make a profit, and achieve life balance. When I started at age sixteen, I had no idea how to run a business. Thirty (something) years later I am still learning not only how to run a business, but also be a mom, a wife, a friend, a boss, and just maybe, if I have time, have a life. I have hired business coaches, attended seminars on social media, purchased DVDs, and attended all day retreats. I STRONGLY RECOMMEND that future entrepreneurs get outside help, but there's a lot of bad, and very expensive, information out there.

The Do's and Don'ts of Starting a Private Counseling Practice

Here's the main DOs and DON'Ts I have learned:

Don't:

- **Assume the expensive stuff is better than the less-expensive stuff.** The two best seminars I ever attended were the least expensive. Zig Zigler hosted an event in San Antonio when I graduated from college in 1989 and for less than one hundred dollars I got to hear him, Barbara Bush, and several other major speakers who changed the way I thought about myself and my future. Fast forward twenty years to Dave Ramsey's Financial Peace University. Again, for around one hundred dollars, I got to participate in a truly life-changing business paradigm-shifting experience.

- **Purchase the biggest package.** Most gurus worth their salt have tons of free stuff. Try those first to see if they are what you need, then purchase.

- **Sign the consultant contract.** Most business consultants will understand you are not working with a lot of capital. As a new entrepreneur when you sign a contract, the money should be coming IN not going out.

Do:

- **Get to know your guru.** Thanks to social media you can listen to podcasts, view Twitter feeds, and read free book excerpts. Get to know before you buy.

- **Follow directions.** One of the things I remember about Dave Ramsey's course is his statement, "If you follow this plan you will get out of debt. If you don't, you won't." He was right. If you are going to purchase the material then…

- **Go all in.** If you have tested it, followed it, asked the questions, and gotten as many freebies as possible and you have decided to follow through with a purchase, then follow directions! If your guru says jump and you say, "well, I'm more of a swimmer," then you have only yourself to blame if things don't work out.

Becoming an entrepreneur will be the hardest job you ever love. This chapter explains a few things I've learned, but they're guidelines at best, not rules. I strive to provide the best information at affordable prices so follow me on social media (Facebook Kate Walker Training, Twitter @drk8d, and my blog at www.katewalkertraining.com) ask me questions, test me, and try out my free stuff. In the end if you are having fun, turning a profit, and becoming the best counselor you can possibly be, then that's what it's all about.

> **Ask yourself...**
>
> - If I want to have a private practice, am I ready to be equipped as an entrepreneur?
> - What legal advice do I need in setting up a LLC?
> - Who do I need to network with?
> - How do I effectively market?
> - How do I make money?

Nuts and Bolts

How do you start a private practice? What are the first steps? What are the next steps? The nuts and bolts of private practice are important because this will be the foundation for the systems that will keep your practice running smoothly. This chapter is not legal advice. I am not a lawyer and I don't play one on the internet. These are things that I have done, my experts have done, and it has worked out. Please consult your favorite attorney before executing anything related to laws and business.

This "Nuts and Bolts" section is divided into:

- Formation
- Networking and marketing
- Money
- Risk management
- Amazing client experience

Formation

First and foremost, you need a separation of your business and your private assets. Think of it this way. When a problem happens (someone trips and falls, files a complaint, sues you for malpractice) do you want them to walk away with your practice assets, or all of your assets? Let's face it, counseling is one of the lowest-overhead startups you will find. Used couch, rented office space, new computer, and a chair. Bam! Open for business for around three to five thousand dollars. In Texas, a "DBA" or "Doing business as" designation will only protect your business name and help you open a bank account; it won't protect your house and your car if the worst happens. I created an LLC called "All About the Family LLC" to create an entity separate from my personal assets. From there, I created two 'dba' entities:

achievebalance.org and Kate Walker Training. Ann's Place is a special Texas non-profit entity apart from All About the Family. In theory, if I get sued and the plaintiff's lawyer manages to beat mine, he or she will walk away with my malpractice insurance (one million/three million), a used sofa, and a ten-year old Dell Computer. My home, cars, retirement accounts, and other assets are safe.

As I mentioned earlier, counselors typically have low startup costs. Don't get your business formation documents and advice (or your website) from the LLC bargain bin. You can cut costs in lots of other places, but those areas are the ones to splurge on. I'm a big believer in "mistakes make you stronger" and "you can come back from almost anything" but doing it right the first time is important because mistakes and do-overs in the formation stage cost time and money. Also, they add stress, which increases anxiety and diminishes your ability to make good decisions.

Networking and Marketing, or Building Compassion and Outreach into Your Private Practice

As you consider how you will build a private practice, you must think about how you will market or advertise that you exist. Next to money, this is by far the biggest complaint I hear from future and current private practice owners. Why? Probably because we are all a bunch of introverts who work best one-on-one. That's our gift and our skill set. The problem? If you don't advertise you are robbing the world of your talent.

The best example I can think of to make this point is your local dentist. She probably puts her flyers and brochures out at the local physician's office or the bank. You probably walk past those "marketing" materials ten times without even noticing they are there. The eleventh time, however, you have a toothache. In true Gestalt fashion, the background becomes the foreground and before you know it you are fumbling with your phone to take a picture of the material so you can Google her website. By the time you reach the car you have already made an appointment online and have the directions laid out in Google maps.

Did marketing work? Absolutely. You had pain, you noticed the marketing material at the right time, you visited the professional and achieved relief. That's why at *achievebalance.org* we don't call it marketing, we call it compassion and outreach. You have a gift to help people with their pain. If people in pain can't find you, that's a problem. Good marketing means you are easy to find, easy to contact, and easy to schedule with. You have an obligation as a talented compassionate counselor to make sure you place your compassion and outreach materials in view of those who need it most.

Counseling is a pain-based business. People notice us when they can't tolerate their pain anymore. Individuals can have very high pain tolerances. In fact, they probably won't seek a solution outside of their comfort zone until the pain has impacted their relationships, their health, their job/school performance, or their freedom. So how can you as a therapist make sure you are the one that comes to mind when an individual experiences a mental 'toothache?'

1. **Expand your circle of influence (also called 'Networking').** Don't get scared by the word influence, simply think of it like the shampoo commercial in the '80s – "They will tell two friends, then they will tell two friends, and so on, and so on." The more people you meet and impact in a positive way, the more people will recommend you to friends and loved ones.

2. **Join Toastmasters.** Guess what? Writing another article or newsletter will not get you a new client this week. Getting out into the community and talking about you and your services will! If you are an introvert there are smaller more structured groups you can join. Toastmasters can help you develop your confidence so you can tell someone exactly what you do and

how you can help them with their pain. If you are an extrovert, then you should already have a talk or speech ready to go that you can give at a moment's notice.

3. **Practice 5 – 2 – 1.** Contact five new people and tell them about you and your practice. Refer two people to someone else (this is the law of give and you shall receive) and send one thank you to one of your referral sources. Start by making this a weekly goal that becomes a daily habit.

Learn How to Manage, Steward, Make, Wisely Spend and Invest Money

My friend Kim and I would meet at a local coffee shop once or twice a month. She owned a business that specialized in tutoring kids; I owned a business that specialized in counseling families. We didn't meet to talk about our clients though; we met in order to talk about business. By the way, "talking about business" is code for "let's talk about ways we can make more money."

Not long into our regular meetings I told her how uncomfortable counselors are about making money. She looked at me like I was crazy.

"Why would making money be a bad thing?" she asked.

"I'm not sure," I said. "Counselors just look at each other weird if one of them talks about making more money."

She was still looking at me like I was crazy.

"Look," I said, "Counselors help people by keeping secrets. We listen, they talk, and if we see them on the street we pretend not to know them. It's like we're priests without collars. I'm not Catholic but I think priests take a vow of poverty. Maybe that's why it's so hard for counselors to talk about making money."

After that conversation we made a point of sitting down with our coffee and taking off our "pretend collars" so we could talk about money. It actually helped me.

What's up with counselors and money? I'm not a priest. I did not take a vow of poverty. In fact, I have three kids and I am an equal wage earner in my home. Why did "priest" (priestess?) resonate with me? I tried to put my thumb on it and it might have been a message I learned in grad school. Or maybe it was the time when one of our local professors was walking with one of our University interns through my offices and was overheard saying, "Don't expect to have offices like this when you go out into the world. Practices like this are a fluke."

A fluke?

Darn it, someone forgot to tell me!

As I meditate on those truths that we counselors hold to be self-evident, I can't help but wonder what happened to the counselor private practice owner. Most of us who graduated from a counseling program received little to no business education. Because of that, while we are pursuing life, liberty, and happiness we are simultaneously struggling with finances, time, and burnout. I was going to list *The Counselor's Bill of Rights*, but instead I came up with...

The Counselor's List of Exceptions

1. Everyone gets sick and must take time off from work to heal, "Except the private practice owner - if she takes a sick day she will not make money."

2. We will all slow down or retire as we age and become less physically able, "Except the private practice owner – he shall work until he dies because he lives off of everything he makes and the rest goes to taxes."

3. Savings accounts will be used to fix things when they break, "Except the private practice owner – since she has no savings (see number 2) she will have to max out her credit cards when the air conditioner finally goes out."

This list is ***not*** okay!

Making enough money to feed yourself and your family, take a day off, eventually retire, and fix things when they break are reasonable expectations for any job. As a private practice owner we do this first and foremost by charging our clients. Confidently communicating what to charge your clients for your services is important and consistency correlates with fairness. Most codes state that you must have your rate in your service contract and if you decide to change that rate, you must do it in writing. Charging different amounts, allowing some clients to "wait to pay" or waiving fees altogether for different clients without using a consistent tool like the federal poverty standards can seem discriminatory. Communicating the therapeutic use of money helps your clients understand accountability and the value of your time.

Along with communicating a consistent fee, it is vital to focus on filling your schedule. Filling your schedule is important because a full schedule allows you to project income and plan your weekly and monthly budget. Expect 10-15 percent attrition each week. My secrets?

- *I work long Mondays*. Because of our strict cancelation policy, I can reliably take in at least 50 percent of my client income for the week on that day. Since I have already planned for some attrition, by Friday if I have clients who need to reschedule or cancel, it doesn't throw off my monthly budget. I can fill those slots with emergency clients, wait-listed clients, or just take the hour off and work on paperwork or marketing.

- *I always have three slots over my target available each week.* So again, if my target is twenty clients, I will have twenty-three slots available. Then when my 10-15 percent attrition hits, I have still filled my schedule and my budget is intact.

In addition to your client income, another solution to the "money problem" is to develop multiple streams of income. These other income sources will not only provide cash you can use for a rainy day, they can fund a retirement account, or provide investment capital for your growing business. Here are examples of four streams of income so your business keeps working even if you need a day off:

1. **Your supportive partner's income.** If you have a partner who supports you in your business endeavor, then his/her income can be the cushion you will need if you have to step away from work or if an emergency hits.

2. **Don't quit your day job.** If you are trained as a teacher, offer to teach online courses or one day per week at a local university. If you are trained as a musician, offer private lessons or take weekend gigs.

3. **Become a LPC/LMFT Supervisor.** Interns must have 18 months to two years of supervision and the going rate for supervision is anywhere from $40 - $100 per hour.

4. **Monetize your website.** You can join affiliate programs, offer online continuing education, or sell products (as long as you follow your state's laws and ethics codes).

5. **Use interns to deliver affordable counseling to your community in exchange for free supervision.** You receive additional client income when you aren't in your office and your supervisees get free supervision. We have a wonderful model with our Texas non-profit Ann's Place.

At *achievebalance.org* most of us do not take insurance. This allows us to take a smaller number of clients for about the same income. The therapists who do take insurance usually do so temporarily to act as a "bridge" to cash pay. In the end, we spend most of our time and resources on intakes rather than maintaining a census. We don't offer billing resources.

Risk Management

The scene: You are having lunch with a counselor friend and she casually mentions, "Whew! I finally got my continuing education finished! Good thing too because my license renews this month."

You feel a sinking feeling in the pit of your stomach because you too, are renewing your license this month, and you completely forgot about your continuing education hours. You finish the lunch and rush back to your office and enter search terms into Google like, "Fast LPC CE," and "Online Counseling Continuing Education." The same courses come up again and again. One charges to access the material. Another takes precious minutes to load the exam and you notice several mistakes. Still another wants to charge you before you even pass the exam. You absolutely HATE online courses but you bite the bullet and pay your money anyway, vowing that next time, you will get your CEs in person.

Not a good start to managing risk.

If you followed my example in the formation stage you have already taken some solid steps toward managing risks you will encounter running a private practice. You can't stop there; however, as a licensed counselor and business owner you must weave risk management into your everyday systems.

1. **Read the licensure laws. A LOT.** I am always amazed at how many LPCs and LMFTs have not read ALL the laws governing their license! When you read the laws you will discover your

scope of practice. The code outlines how you may advertise your services, your continuing education requirements, how to respond to critical situations, and what to include in your service agreement/consent to treat. It is not uncommon for laws to be added and changed yearly so make this a habit.

2. **Join a consultation group.** I know, I know. You don't have time. Groups are held during prime therapy time. You can't afford to give up the client revenue. You know what? Make time! An accountability group will help you attain your goals and stay legal and ethical. I challenge you to make this a priority.

3. **Understand, and clearly be able to explain, how you help.** Counselors are highly skilled professionals trained in the art of emotional pain relief. We use our skills to promote insight in our clients so they feel better. When they feel better, we terminate treatment. If they don't feel better, then we look at our treatment plan and make adjustments. If we make adjustments and our clients are still not feeling better, we help them find a specialist who can meet their needs and hopefully accomplish what we could not. At achievebalance.org and Ann's Place beginning with the first phone call, we clearly explain what a potential client can expect from counseling. If you have difficulty explaining how you help and what you will do/how you will refer if and when counseling is no longer helpful, then you must learn.

4. **Plan for growth.** You will not always have a small practice. Once the community learns you can help with pain you will grow. How will you handle returning phone calls? How will you handle additional file storage? Who can you refer to if your practice gets too big? Who can help your current clients if you have an emergency or need to go out of town for a few

days? Planning for growth is important because it is inevitable. Don't be surprised by it.

5. **If you grow to the point you have interns or staff, incorporate a policy and procedures manual and a progressive discipline plan.** In Texas, both LPC and LMFT codes state you must remediate an intern/associate before you fire them. If you have staff and you need to fire someone, you must document your efforts to evaluate and discipline before you fire them or you could run into problems. What is a remediation plan? What is a good evaluation? What is a progressive discipline plan? All of these things start with a good contract. At achievebalance.org and Ann's Place we have a yearly orientation and training everyone must attend in order to continue seeing clients. We review the policy and procedures and renew our HIPAA training. It's a great way to acclimate new folks into the culture of our business and sets a base line expectation for everyone.

Amazing Client Experience

Clients come to us exhausted because they can no longer cope with their pain. This exhaustion is much like putting down a weight after carrying it for too long, or asking for help with a heavy load of groceries that you are about to drop.

Helping clients overcome their exhaustion
and creatively solve their own problems
is one of the greatest services
we as therapists can execute and the joy of our career.

Unfortunately, in private practice, problems can happen. Exhausted clients aren't always amenable to your scheduling SNAFUs, long wait times, and phone tag. Helping your clients have an amazing experience is important not only because it just makes sense, but also because studies show clients who are satisfied with your service, even if they still have an emotional issue, are less likely to file complaints.

When we do our yearly orientation meeting at achievebalance.org, we talk about our five core values. There are three that focus specifically on an amazing client experience:

Our Core Values

- The minute the client walks through the door, they are welcomed with respect, warmth, and kindness.

- Remember we're not selling a technique, a degree, or a specialty. Our clients come to us for relief from their pain and we are committed to helping.

- Whether our client is a family of one, two, or five we are committed to providing unconditional positive regard, and dedicated to providing a solution focused plan and a goal oriented roadmap.

- Clients are strong! We believe that our clients come to us with strength and they own the keys to solving their own problems. They won't need you for long if you are helping them discover those strengths.

- Focus on growing your intakes NOT maintaining the same client load week after week. Fostering client dependency is unethical!

Providing clients with an amazing experience means serving them quickly. If your potential clients call you and they can't get in to see you or talk to you the same week, then you probably need to add a reliable referral to your practice. It also means giving them a plan starting with the first session. If you were visiting your dentist for extensive dental work would you leave the first appointment without knowing the treatment plan? Would you be satisfied if he told you "I think you will be seeing me for a while," but didn't tell you how and when your work would be finished? Help your clients understand what to expect after three sessions, whether or not you assign homework, if you allow other family members into a session, and how they will know if working with you will be a good fit.

Finally, accommodate their needs and provide expert service. Sick kids and traffic jams happen. Can your clients use the phone to call you for a session if they can't make it in? How many hours of continuing education in couple therapy have you actually completed? Do you know the dynamics of infidelity? Become the expert in your field. Your clients deserve that.

Owning a private practice will lead to the same emotions you would experience opening up any business. Most of your work initially is spent building the brand, creating systems, and marketing. Long hours are part of the job (just ask my husband!) and the economy ups and downs can make for a not-so-thrilling roller coaster. I recommend you start reading entrepreneur literature like *Success* magazine and *Business Insider* (online app) to get a feel for the entrepreneur life. If you can keep your job while building a practice, great. If not, then build a bridge so you can make it through the one to three-year building process (see building a financial bridge in chapter five).

There are lots of public domain (free) books and community resources you can try. Our local community college has a Small Business Development Department. I also recommend you contact other therapists in successful private practices and ask questions.

 **Next Steps…**

This chapter is overflowing with practical advice for starting and maintaining a private counseling practice. Skim back through the chapter and find the 10 most important things you need to do or do

better that you have learned or re-learned in this chapter. Then head to the "Resources" page to unlock templates, examples, and more at www.mynextstepsbook.com.

1. _____
2. _____
3. _____
4. _____
5. _____
6. _____
7. _____
8. _____
9. _____
10. _____

Here is what the Experts have to say about other streams of income, private practice advice, and their "secret sauce."

Do you have another stream of income?

Jean: *Not at this time. Unless you count my side job, the IOP, which wouldn't give me much…My husband's job, of course. One thing I've thought about doing is creating workbooks that people can download, and I could charge for. It seems really pretty easy to put together.*

Janet: *I recently published a book called "Stepping Stones to a Healthy Stepfamily." The other thing is my equine therapy business that I incorporated 11 years ago, so that's another stream of income. Then my placement and consulting* *services, that's a little bit different stream of income, and then the career assessment and testing. Those are the streams of income for me.*

Christopher: *Definitely teaching… also we do some consulting work. We do some child observation work as well for high-profile divorce cases. For a while, I was running Dallas County's Family Drug Court program until they decided to pull the funding for the program, so we let it go, which was sad because that was part of my dissertation too. There was a nonprofit we were running for a while too, but we let that go.*

Nonprofits are so difficult! And getting people to give money, and give money regularly…I was the director of operations, I wasn't even in fundraising, and I felt like all I was doing was fundraising the whole time. But now, our main source of income really is just our counseling income. My goal over the next two years, is to just streamline it all to where there's only one source of income, and then teaching just for fun.

Cheryl: *Kind of like the retirement piece, my husband's income has always been our primary income. Also, I used to teach. Even when I taught, my income was something that we saved aside for colleges and for just future savings. Now, we have purchased the building that I practice in, so we lease that space and that's an extra stream of income. I guess rental property is another source of additional income.*

Kate: *My other streams of income include my live and online courses at Kate Walker Training, my income from teaching at SHSU, and my husband's income. Supervising interns,* *freelancing as a musician, and my non-profit Ann's Place are just ways for me to give back and have fun.*

What are two or three pieces of advice you would give someone going into private practice?

Christopher: *So, the first one, which I think everyone laughs at a little bit, but you know my experience as a board member, and just my experience as a professional, don't have sex with your clients.*

That's number one. Number two is show up on time. I can't tell you how many therapists I've known that just didn't show up to a session, or a student that just didn't show up. I actually had a practicum student one time talk about how he thought his Saturday client wasn't going to come, so he went to go look at cars, and I'm like are you kidding me? Then, we almost fired an employee because she failed to call in to say that she was going to the hospital because she was sick. She had a client she didn't show up for, and it was a new client. We didn't know what happened, so it looked like she's causing harm to the client. Just be there. If you have a session at 4:00, be there at 3:55. It is not that hard.

I can't tell you how many times I've had people come in for interviews, where we've had an interview to hire somebody at 4:00, and they don't get there until 4:05. I just cancel the interview. If you can't get here on time, how can I trust you to treat a client well? You know, that's the most basic simple task out there, how can you not do that? And if you just do that, adhere to the person-centered model... showing up is the major part, just being there...clients want somebody to talk to. And if everyone in their life, is ignoring them or doesn't show up for them, and you don't show up, I mean that will cause harm.

That's a big piece of advice that I like to give them. The third one is something from personal experience that really is just kind of one of my core values. Don't assume. Just don't make assumptions. I hate it when administrative staff says, oh, we "assumed that…". I immediately ask "what is our number one rule? We do not assume." It just gets you into trouble. Someone says, "I assumed because their card said Blue Cross Blue Shield that they actually had Blue Cross Blue Shield health insurance, or medical, or mental health insurance," which they didn't. They had Magellan, and now we're four weeks behind on payment, or something. Small assumptions can create big problems.

Yeah, in fact I tell everybody, I would rather you ask me 10 dumb questions a day than make one bad assumption… Because I can answer an email, I can do a text message very quickly. I am very responsive. You know, that's one of our core values at Taylor Counseling Group; we have our response time down for new clients to within 15 minutes on an initial inquiry. If you make an inquiry between 7:00 AM and 10:00 PM, you will get a response back within 15 minutes, or less.

We pride ourselves on that, and so we pride ourselves on being very, very reliable, and reachable, and accessible. And so if you have a dumb question, like "I don't remember which folder this goes in," I would much rather you ask that question now, so I can just say, "Hey, it's the green folder," and just be done with it. That way it's done correctly versus somebody who's auditing your account, and we find out 10 weeks later that this wasn't done properly, and so it wasn't billed correctly, or, we billed for the wrong amount, and we actually should've collected an extra $100 on this case, and we didn't.

Cheryl: *The first one I suggest is, when you're starting out you're most likely trying to build a clientele and trying to create a name for yourself, so I would suggest that to connect in your community and to find a way to offer something at little to no cost so that you can be a resource to the community and you can get to know people. I did a lot of pre-marriage counseling, and I also did parenting classes at CISC at no charge. I was so thankful to be there, and then able to get to know people and be a referral source in the future. So that would be the first one.*

The second one is have an organized plan or flowchart for systems. So whether it's your system of how you return phone calls or whether it's a system of how you do scheduling or a system for how you do billing. And I know that everyone's systems could look different, but if you're going to start your own private practice, you have to know your system.

For example, I used to be terrible at returning phone calls. I only worked part time, and the other three days a week I was at home with my kids. I would wait four days to return the phone call because I was at home and not working, and that's not efficient, especially if you're trying to build a business. It's not good for the clients, because they need to hear back from somebody. I moved to an online scheduling system where my voicemail actually has a link to schedule, so that if someone leaves me a message, they also have a way to schedule an appointment. Some people are in crisis and they want to schedule and get it on the calendar right then and there. So that helped a lot. My scheduling system is now, I still return phone calls, but not as timely as I'd love it to be. I'd love it to be within a day, but if I don't, at least they're able to schedule online.

The third one is just the accountability piece to clients. I know when I started, I was so eager to have clients, and so excited to have clients and to help that oftentimes I was willing to just maybe lower standards, lower expectations, and not hold clients accountable as much. So, if they didn't show, I would tell them, "no worries, just come whenever you can." I also had this wide-open schedule, "Come whenever you want." And I had appointments at Monday at 9 and then Wednesday at 7, and it was all over the place. It wasn't allowing me to have any peace in my own space, so I narrowed in the walls of when I was available. I became a little bit firm of, "Here are my appointments. Which one would work for you?" And then the accountability piece to clients was valuable. They really received it a lot better than I thought that they would. I was afraid that I would turn away business, but I think it actually helped the business grow. Time and money are our resources.

Katherine: *The first one is get educated. If you're a woman, find a women's business center at the Small Business Administration. If you're not, then find a Small Business Administration regional development center in your area. Find a place that is designed to help educate small business owners on the infrastructure of a business. What are the forms that you need to fill out to incorporate yourself appropriately? What paperwork do you need to file on an annual basis in terms of taxes at the state and federal level? So that's the first piece of advice; go educate yourself on the business regulations that you need to know about, so you don't end up in jail because you just didn't.*

The second piece is get a freakin' CPA. Oh my God, get a CPA. I don't know why counselors think that they don't have to be business people, but we have to be business people. I just came out of a two-hour continuing ed session, and that was the big takeaway. Healthcare has changed so much that mental health professionals who don't understand the business side of the industry are going to get pushed out of the industry. We have to become more business-savvy. We have to understand that there is a business side to helping people, and the biggest piece of that is the money management. So, get a CPA for God's sake, get a CPA.

The third piece would be get mentorship. Find someone, find a couple of people that have maybe not a whole lot more experience than you, but a little bit more experience than you so that you can ask them questions about how do you find a space for your practice? What should it look like? How do you find help? Do you need help? How do you market yourself? Like all of these things, I see time and time again, counselors failing at a private practice because they think all I have to do is get a space, and that might mean in an office building on the fifth floor, or that might mean a website. But they think that's all they have to do, and then all of a sudden, they're just going to be inundated with all the clients they need to make the money they need in order to support themselves. Not be like a corporate giant that has millions and millions in revenue, but just enough to make ends meet. Counselors fail at having a private practice, over and over again, because they don't understand the business side of it.

So those are my three pieces…Find a women's business center. Find a small business development center. Get some free education on establishing a business to protect yourself and your family, and all your personal liabilities. Get a CPA, and then get some mentorship.

Jean: *Be courageous, take chances. Be patient and long standing, and be open and receptive to change and growth. I have had eight years to experience all of these things.*

I think the one that really stood out the most for me is be patient because like any of us, I want it, and I want it now. I want the big office now, I want the full caseload now, I want the challenging cases that I can actually help now. And it doesn't ever look like that. So be patient. Let it develop. But it's very hard. Oh, and number four, or maybe number five. Don't compare. Because we're all doing that, right? We're all doing the same thing. We own this business, right? It's our baby and we have to take care of it. So there's all this investment in it, too. It takes a lot of guts to be an entrepreneur. It takes a lot of courage. So there is going to be worry… how do I know there's abundance and that there'll be enough.

Janet: *Okay. I love that question because when I have people that come and interview me for the field of psychology, these are some of the things that I tell them. First, I tell them work in a psychiatric hospital. You will see the best of the best and the worst of the worst, and you get to see how medicine works, you get to see how psychiatrists work. I actually had the gift of working in a psychiatric hospital and cutting my teeth there before managed care came on board. Now it's very short term; so like I said, you will walk away so confident after you've worked in a psychiatric hospital because you see everything. I always encourage people to work there part of the time.*

> *Then I also encourage people to speak. Get good at a topic or two, and go out and share and network. You're helping other people, you're teaching them, and you're letting people see you, because a lot of times people do not trust going to a therapist, and other professionals won't refer to a therapist until they've heard them speak and they hear them in person, so be willing to put yourself out there and share your gift of speaking even if you're scared to do it. Impart wisdom to others.*
>
> *The other thing that I encourage people to do is to step out and do something different and just keep learning. Do not stop learning, and that's what I love about this field is that ten years from now, we're going to know so much more. Five years from now, we're going to know…so keep learning.*

Kate: *My advice? Listen to these experts and do what they say!*

What's your secret sauce?

Jean: *Is it my morning routine? No, I'm on Facebook for about an hour while I'm drinking my coffee in the morning. My brand of coffee? Maybe. So, I started thinking that maybe it is my style. I have a style about me, and I think I use that in my private practice. I use it in my life, too. I like to express myself. I'm not the most extroverted person, so I use my clothing and things like that to help me express myself for people to know me without me having to say anything, which is hard. I think I do that in my practice, as well. I help my clients know me by how I dress. I do it intentionally. I want to help my clients with their identities, to branch out a little bit, or to really help them step into who they are and know that it's a good thing. I think I am conscious of that … owning who I am.*

So, the clearer I can be in who I am, which is what I teach my clients, the clearer my practice becomes. To live that way has helped clarify what my intentions and goals are instead of the other way around. It's evolution.

Katherine: *Piggybacking off the books that I found helpful on HRD, those books have helped us create a culture. It's the culture. The secret sauce is the culture of the organization…that's helped it be successful. We have had feasts and famine, so there were times when I had to personally float payroll, and then the next month, we still didn't get our reimbursement, you know, our billing, and I couldn't afford to float payroll a second month in a row, and I had to tell the staff, sorry, you didn't know it, but I floated payroll last month. Well, we still haven't gotten our reimbursement. We don't have the money to support payroll this month, and I don't have the money to float it this month, I am sorry.*

You know, so we've had these really tough times financially, where we couldn't make the rent, and we're having to pay late fees for not paying rent on time. But being transparent with the team and fostering a culture where the team feels like they're committed regardless of when things are bad, and they are still committed. It's the culture, the climate that I bring to the table. We try really hard to foster this within the whole organization. And when things are great, you know, we don't get bit in the head. And when we happen to have conversations about, okay, we're being very successful, right now, but let's remember there will be times when we're not, so we have to stay grounded, and stay committed. And so the secret sauce is the culture and the vision that I have, the culture that I want, and it's really helped tremendously.

Cheryl: *I also love to meet other therapists, and okay so this is not at the sauce level yet, but maybe close, I love to help people find referrals. So, I love the notion, kind of the abundance theory, that if a client doesn't see me, then they'll find the right therapist, and I love helping them find that therapist. I think, in the end, that's actually helped me gain clients because they see that I'm willing to be a helper. If I'm not a good fit for them, then I'll help them find a good fit, so maybe it's just my willingness to help, to be a resource..*

Christopher: *My secret sauce is actually pretty complex. I can give you the PowerPoint, if you'd like (laughing). We run a program called "EOS," I just mentioned the book, "The Entrepreneurial Operating System," which is a nine-part plan that we have put together. Our company operates in a very specific way, where we have different departments. We have a support staff, operations, management. We have quarterly meetings, where we all get together to discuss what the significant problems have been for that quarter*

Each employee has a number that they have to meet by the end of the week, whether that number is zero emails left to respond to, or acquisition of four new clients, or treatment of 15 clients that week or 20 clients that week, whatever their unique number is. And we call these rocks, these are things that they have to do every day to gain traction to move the company forward.

And then, we have a three-year goal, a five-year goal, and a 10-year goal, and we are just very diligent in maintaining those goals. We have core values for the company, and we have a really strong sense of teamwork at Taylor Counseling Group, so I think that's probably a big component to our success. All the therapists are salaried employees. They get more benefit from helping everyone else because as the practice does better, they all do better, and they all rise up together. And so whereas if it's just five of us in an office, and we all have different practices, there's really no incentive for me to help you other than we just share an office space, and it's probably good that we like each other.

In our system, you have office hours that you're being paid for to consult with your fellow members, to consult with your team, and to make sure everyone's ok, and to kind of bring everyone up together, so that's been a good component.

Janet: *I think my secret sauce is I just genuinely care about people. I genuinely care about people and their lives, and I feel like it is such a gift that people will come in and trust me enough to share with me. I always find that a miracle. I really do.*

Kate: *My secret sauce has to be my supportive family and village. There's no way I could do half of what I've done if my husband and kids didn't support my efforts. When my parents were alive they would watch my kids. When my parents couldn't help, my church and my friends would be there. It takes a village to raise an entrepreneur.*

Ok, Dear Reader, what is your secret sauce?

_____

_____

_____

Final Word

THE LASTING BENEFITS OF BEING A COUNSELOR

Being a counselor is easy, fun, and rewarding? Right? Not all the time, but I designed this book to provide you with next steps and to keep you from quitting when the going gets tough. And it will get tough. Whether you are looking for a counseling career that channels your passion or you are a counselor who has lost your passion, this book is your foundation, so you can get what you need to keep going. Now you have the right blocks for building a satisfying counseling career. Now you know experts and EXACTLY how they succeed so you don't have to re-invent the wheel. If you read all, or even some, of the chapters you are probably motivated to ask more questions, do some research on the Google machine, or find out more specific steps so you can take action.

The benefits of more specific steps in moving forward with the career you love are obvious: don't re-invent the wheel. If you can find paperwork that someone is already using in their successful private practice, then ask if it is okay to adapt it to your practice. If someone has scripts that help you answer the phones in a way that helps clients choose your services, then ask if you can borrow them. If you can find routines, hacks, habits, or lists that save you time and energy so you can focus on finishing your hours, finishing your degree, providing amazing service to your clients, or building your private practice then don't procrastinate; start incorporating them into your daily routine today!

More specific steps are important because this book painted a picture in broad strokes; it didn't give a lot of detail. Be diligent in your research and take time to find good information.

- Postgraduate next steps are important because you can waste a lot of time and money if you don't follow the correct procedures to become licensed.

- Private practice next steps are important because you need to avoid costly mistakes.

- Internship next steps are important because a bad internship experience can impact your entire counseling career.

Some other topics I did not cover in this book include:

- How to create a private practice retirement plan. This is an important detail that should be a part of everyone's success visualization.

- The pros and cons of a part-time private practice. Part-time private practices are great for people with kids, retirees who have a fixed income and just want to fill the "gaps" and school counselors who want a private practice experience. It is important to know the key components so that your part-time private practice stays truly part-time (and doesn't become a full-time pain in the neck).

- Actual phone answering scripts, budget templates, and a three point wrap up we use at the end of every third or fourth session as an assessment tool. These elements are the "secret sauce" of achievebalance.org and Ann's Place and have been keys to providing our clients with an amazing therapeutic experience.
- How to navigate the summer slump and fluctuations in the economy when you have your own private practice.

Starting your counseling career will lead to some of the same emotions you would experience starting any new venture. You remember those feelings? That rush of confusion and excitement when you walked on to your first college campus; the joy and fear when you walked down the aisle; that unnamable feeling in your gut when you signed the contract at your first "real job." It will be like that.

If you choose private practice, most of your work initially will be spent building the brand, creating systems, and marketing. If you are in your internship, long hours are part of the job. If you are changing careers to become a counselor and you can keep your job while you get started, great. If not, then build a bridge so you can make it through the lean times.

What's the bottom line?

Don't quit.

Your story sparked something in you that gave you a calling to relieve pain in others. Don't let the bumps in the road throw you off course. The world needs you to be a counselor and embrace the career you love.

Parting words from our experts:

Cheryl: *Doing private practice counseling is one of the best businesses ever, and it's been one of the best moves for my* *family, just schedule-wise and the ability to impact the community and have a source of income. It's been great. So if you're afraid of it, don't be afraid. Just reach out and meet people and connect with people and it can be wonderful.*

Christopher: *I'm a big fan of Henry David Thoreau, so I would just say go to the woods. That's what I tell everybody, go to the woods. "I went to the woods because I wished to live deliberately, to front only the essential facts of life, and see if I could not learn what it had to teach." I think it's just really good advice. I just tell people to go to the woods, whenever possible.*

Katherine: *I don't know what it's like to have children and have a private practice, but I have a spouse who supports me, so he understands it, and he's all in, and he helps me.*

Janet: *I think this is an amazing field. There is never a dull moment in this field, and like I said, from what I've seen from 1989 to 2017 has just been incredible, and now with even more technology and more that we're understanding about DNA and genetics, I think it is going to explode in the field of psychology and affect how we practice. It's just going to be so exciting to see what happens in the next five to ten or fifteen years. There's just so much to look forward to and so much ahead, so it's an exciting, exciting field.*

About the Author

Kate Walker, PhD is a Licensed Professional Counselor Supervisor and a Licensed Marriage and Family Therapist Supervisor with offices in The Woodlands, Texas. Dr. Walker started Kate Walker Training in 2015 after working alongside her mentor Dr. Judy DeTrude from 2007 until Judy's retirement in 2014. Together, they trained hundreds of Texas counselors through their practice achievebalance.org offering courses such as the forty-hour supervision course, online counselor continuing education, and face to face seminars.

Today, Kate is an active advocate for counselors, supervisors, and counselor educators. She has served as a member of the Sam Houston State University Doctoral Advisory Board, taught master's level counseling students at SHSU as an adjunct professor, and was the Director of Clinical Field Experience at the University of Houston Victoria. She was elected 2015-2016 President of the Texas Association for Counselor Education and Supervision (TACES) and currently serves as the TACES LPC Board Liaison. An avid researcher, she has been a speaker and presenter at the Texas Counseling Association Annual Conference, the Texas Association of Marriage and Family Therapy Annual Conference, and the Texas Association for Counselor Education and Supervision National Conference. Kate earned her master's degree and PhD from Sam Houston State University. She earned her Bachelor of Music degree from The University of Texas at Austin and taught orchestra in the public schools for thirteen years. She continues to freelance as a professional bass player for singer/songwriters in the Houston area.

Kate has a husband David, three amazing kids, Kyle, Ridgley, and Sarah, a German shepherd, two cats, and three turtles.

CONTACT INFORMATION:

www.mynextstepsbook.com and www.katewalkertraining.com

Look for other books in the *My Next Steps* series:

Create a Private Practice You'll Love

Write Your Book

Resources

Head to www.mynextstepsbook.com and enter the passcode "nextlevel" to access the following free resources:

Lists:

- Steps to become a licensed professional counselor or marriage and family therapist in Texas
- Steps to become a LPC/LMFT Supervisor in Texas
- Steps to start a counseling practice
- CACREP - accredited counselor education programs in Texas

From the Experts:

- Favorite and Recommended Books
- Favorite quotes
- Secret Sauce

Links:

- Texas LPC Board
- Texas LMFT Board
- ACA Code of Ethics
- Federal Poverty Standards (to create an ethical sliding fee scale)

Worksheets:

- Counseling Career Success: Visualize and Optimize
- Practice Expenses Calculator
- Kate's Weekly Schedule

Templates and Scripts:

- Policy and Procedures Manual
- Explain How You Help: 10 Minute Potential Client Consultation

www.ingramcontent.com/pod-product-compliance
Lightning Source LLC
Chambersburg PA
CBHW052057110526
44591CB00013B/2250